THE AMERICAN TEENAGER

NICK UMBARGER

The American Teenager by Nick Umbarger

Copyright © 2021 Nick Umbarger

Cover Design By Vivien Reis

ISBN: 978-1-7374185-4-2

Printed in the United States

Table of Contents

Dedication

This book is dedicated to the people who I've met over the years and some who I have yet to meet. My family and friends have a great influence on how I wanted to go about writing this, just so they got the full satisfaction of seeing how they impacted my life one way or another. If it wasn't for my high school English teacher, Mr. Acebo, proposing this last unique literary assignment, I probably wouldn't have sat down and thought about all my good and bad times and turned it into a book.

I want to dedicate this to those who feel like their accomplishments are limited by what they are told.

Because this book is proof they are not...

Introduction

It's quite incredible how this book came to be because I sure am not the person to create something of this magnitude. But there are reasons bigger than I can comprehend that led to the result of this book. Growing up I hated reading, hated writing, everything about literature, and the education system did not align with my interests. I never understood why I did so well in those classes but hated every second of it. In my senior year English class, when I originally got the end of the year assignment, I felt much different about writing.

It was my chance to focus on the practical and life-reflecting moments that I could get an easy grade for. It ultimately became the precursor to this book. I had no intentions of turning the assignment into something bigger than a letter grade, but months passed and I thought about how it would be interesting to expand on it to the point of full public exposure. Meaning that parents and young adults can relate or learn from my experiences from high school. I want to make clear that what I experienced during high school was on a much lower scale compared to some of the wilder stories I heard from others. With that said, I do not condone nor promote any of the activities in this book. I can't tell you how many times I've heard parents wanting to know what goes on in their kids' lives. This could be a transparent perspective for those who want to know what goes on in these early years of life. I hope young adults will find value in my recitation of these stories because there were a few people who I knew that I would want to read about. This also could be a great gathering of stories for those who are well into their later years to understand how generations ahead of them behaved and interacted, a concept I find interesting.

I find it comical how at first I wrote this solely for the purpose of receiving a grade and now it's developed to give hindsight on what goes on in the life of a teenager. It was almost as simple as me waking up one day and deciding to turn it into a book. To me, these stories seem too good to just forget about and go on with life. I had to document some sort of hard copy of these great times. One other reason that I value deeply is having the ability to remember my life events. Time doesn't stop for anyone, and there will be a day where time outlives my memories of some of the greatest times in my life. So when I have more years behind me than ahead, hopefully I don't have to rely on my memory to relive those great moments. That is the true motivation pushing me to write this.

Dean Graziosi, Stefan Aarnio, and Dan Bilzerian inspired me a great amount to write this as well. Stefan was a well-known Canadian businessman who has written many great books and excelled in real estate and life coaching. Dean is also of a similar fashion to business and life coaching. After reading Dean's book *Millionaire Success Habits*, he mentioned a time when he went to write his first book. He gave his first draft to a professional editor and the editor came back to him and said "This is atrocious, you need a whole rewrite" He replied by telling himself I don't need a rewrite because this is exactly how I want people to read this. He fired the editor and got the book published. Dan Bilzerian has had an extreme lifestyle, to say the least, and he's writing a book because of it. Even though my stories are on a much lower scale, him writing about his stories gave me inspiration to write about mine.

I am fortunate to have had a group of people surrounding me with great times and even greater stories. I hope people of all ages find this book of stories entertaining and informative. My purpose is to make it as easy to enjoy reading this as much as I enjoyed writing this. I wrote in a way that as you turn the last page, it's as if you were with me all along the way.

1

Who am I?

L et's start things off with the basics, who am I? I'm not sure if the full extent of that answer can fit on the biggest piece of paper humans can physically develop, but I can try to summarize. In order to have the best understanding of these upcoming stories, you can try to understand who I am. What am I? I'm a guy, a dude, a bro, the XY chromosome, a woman, but without the "wo." A blonde-haired, blue-eyed, left-handed, average-height guy, who thinks if I played connect the dots long enough on myself, it would make out the milky way with every constellation there is.

Nice to meet you, I'm Nick! There are many Nicks in the world, thousands and millions probably, but me, I am one of one. I came into this world on a dark warm night in May at the turn of the century. My fate was more or less in the hands of two people who thought they could raise a child and sure enough, it turned out just fine. four and half years later my sister Rachel was introduced and

I now had a permanent friend to go through life with. I like to be an upstanding brother and fill her in on what the upcoming ages will bring before she reaches them. I'll be that friend that will always be there because there were times where I wish I had that. There is only one guy named Nick who loves skateboarding, cameras, sunsets, hammocking, Oklahoma, and cars! I've always been curious about the world around me and in what ways it continues to fascinate me.

There are many things I cannot live without, I'm not a needy person, but there are some things that make my days so much better. I absolutely cannot live without cars in my life; I truly love them. From a young age, I've always had an interest in them, which is ironic because no one in my family has a taste for modified engines and custom bodywork like I do. I collected a bunch of Hot Wheels, model cars, and posters and fantasized about one day having my own. My neighbor pushed my influence even further, being a few years older than me, he would come home with these loud cars. His friends also had loud cars, which perked my ears every time. Now older and still in love with cars, I see them as an extension of your personality. You can modify anything and everything you want to make them your one-off ride! Just the ability to crank engines up to their full potential is so amazing. I know I'm going to be that guy with more assets in vehicles than real estate!

There's a lot of things I can live without but coffee is towards the bottom of the list. Just one cup every morning does it for me and I'm good for the day. On the days I don't have coffee, I usually have a bad headache for most of the day. Coffee is a funny story when it comes to taste. You can either make your coffee taste like it was squeezed from the earth or add enough sugar to where you're basically drinking a slushie with milk. I can live without a lot of things, but there is one thing that I cannot go without, that being water. Now you may think that's kind of obvious because we would die if we didn't have water. Here's my point, I know many people who rarely drink water and mostly drink only tea or juice. I need water every day. It is the purest form of a liquid that we can physically drink. Water can do nothing but help you in many ways, such as help prevent sickness, keep you hydrated, and it doesn't have sugar, which helps with your teeth and weight. It is just so refreshing and plentiful, I truly could not live without water. Music is also another thing I would have trouble living without. I have a deep appreciation for all sorts of music. As I've grown up, I've noticed a theme that music may be more important to me than I thought. In almost any setting, I can think of a song that relates to my environment or how I'm feeling. I associate songs with many places, events, or people. I enjoy all types of music and that statement doesn't stray too far from a literal sense. I can go from listening to *"Go DJ"* by Lil Wayne, to *"Ashes"* by Celine Dion, to *"House of Wolves"* by Bring Me The Horizon, then to

"Desperado" by Clint Black. I think it's humorous when I think back to when I first developed a taste for a music genre. I had to be around nine years old in the third grade and I would tune my SpongeBob SquarePants radio to the Rap and R&B station, 105.3. I would sit there listening to Jeezy and 50 Cent for hours. I think I was incapable of understanding the lyrics at the time, my parents even warned me that they weren't talking about the best subjects but I remember just falling in love with the beat and rhythm of the genre.

As I got older I began to widen my music range by trying to listen to rock songs, greatly influenced by my dad. Green Day was one of the first rock bands I discovered and enjoyed. I listened to the same 2 genres, Rock and Rap, all the way up until about seventh grade when I really started to like Classic Rock, Electronic Dance Music, and Indie Rock. I began to thoroughly appreciate the context and production of older rock songs along with discovering Indie rock bands, such as The Lumineers, Kodaline, Alt J., and many more. High school is when my taste in music exploded. I can't exactly remember how, but all of a sudden I started liking country music, actively listening to Lana Del Rey, and having an odd obsession with Heavy Metal. I can almost listen to any song nowadays. If I listen to rap I feel like a gangster with diamond chains. If I turn on heavy metal, I'm either extremely mad or hyping up my mood full of energy. When I'm feeling relaxed and mellowed out after a long day, I'll put on The Lumineers, Peach

Pit, or Current Joys. Those bands give me the feeling of carefree happiness.

Classic Rock has a whole different approach on me. When I listen to Classic Rock I tend to feel the most comfortable, like everything is at ease and I can take a step back from everything in the world for a second. In stressful situations, I'll play 70's and 80's music because it is near impossible for those songs to make me feel bad in any way. Obviously, music can make anyone happy and can aid as a temporary escape from the world around them, but I use music to constantly refresh my mood in the setting I'm in. I think it's also interesting to look up some of the lyrics and try to comprehend what the writer is trying to say to their audience, whether that be storytelling, a personal narrative, or more focused on the instruments and computer-generated sounds. I usually listen to classic rock more for the storytelling aspect and how the people writing the song perceived the world at the time. Rap songs statistically do not have as much lyrical authenticity, but tend to focus more on the physical sound of the song to appeal to the listener.

Towards the end of high school, I began to venture out to many branches of the rap genre. Primarily called "Underground," I discovered many artists and sub-genres that captured my liking even more in underground rap. Many of the artists don't talk about positive things, but the main reason I listen to underground rap is that the lyrics and production value are so unique and extreme, I can't find anything like it in any other genre.

I'm a individualistic person. I do things at my own pace, pave my own roads, and do my best to not let any outside factors interfere with my goals. I also like looking after others, as much as I want myself to be in a good place, I want to help others get to one as well. There are times where making others feel good will make you feel good. I practice selflessness whenever I can and reveal empathy to those who need it. But it didn't start like that, everything that's happened in my life has shaped me into who I am today and will continue to be. You'll see in the later stories what events changed me as a person and gave me new perspectives going forward. Every experience in this world is worth learning from and putting in the useful practices that come from them will prove to serve you well. In conclusion of this summary, go USA, God is good, and you can never drink enough water.

2

The Fever Dreams of Childhood

Oklahoma is where my upbringing began and there in my little neighborhood, with a few friends nearby, is where I roamed. I was an explorer in the neighborhood, seeing new things, going over different terrain, and seeing new faces was fascinating to me. I tried to get as familiar as I could with my neighborhood to know the fastest routes to places on my bike to friend's houses and such. Back then it felt like I was Columbus and my neighborhood was the undiscovered land. A kid lived down the street from me named Ben, who was a few grades behind me, but we made friends in school and in the neighborhood. We had many similar interests like exploring, Pokémon, and Nerf guns. He had this big storm drain system that flowed behind his backyard that stretched for a few hundred yards. This became our main source of entertainment and we always would explore the tunnels and catch all sorts of fish nearby.

The main part of this drain tunnel was covered in graffiti and the opening was roughly seven feet in diameter. A concrete canal followed from the opening for about a hundred yards and led to another smaller tunnel that continued through the other side. The other side of this smaller tunnel led out to a cliff-like structure that was about eight feet tall and was made for the water to fall off into the lower part, where it then funneled through small barriers and continued down the stream. At the bottom of the cliff structure was a unique series of terrain. It was like the jungles of the Amazon in the summer and a sandy desert wasteland in the winter. We named this entire structure of water drainage, "the creek."

Right after it would rain for a day or two, the creek would rapidly be flowing and the part where the cliff was, served as a magnificent waterfall I could watch for hours. The mossy build-up at the top, the crashing of water at the bottom, and the overall different ways the water would make its way down from the cliff. One funny part we would mess with was near the waterfall, where there was a small knee-high wall that made the water flow out only in the middle part. When the creek would be flowing for a day or two, it began to pile up sticks and larger debris in the middle flow part. We got so much amusement waiting for it to build up, then taking a large stick or using our hands to clear the dam and watch the water flow twice as fast with twice the volume out into the rest of the stream.

The main opening of the creek tunnel was just the first step of a passageway that seemed to lead into infinity. We were always curious if one day we would decide to explore the great depths of this drain tunnel. Low and behold at some point the endeavor was scheduled to be explored. Ben and I gathered materials like we weren't coming back for months. Stocked up on Gushers, cheese sticks, Grips pouches, water, and a couple of flashlights. With our backpacks loaded and the rest of the day ahead of us, it was time to enter. The first section of the tunnel ran for about 100 yards until it hit a bend. I called this first part "the light section" because it was where the tunnel held the light for about 100 yards in and then when returning back out from the inside you would see light at the bend, no longer needing a flashlight. After passing the initial bend, the second section began. This is the first part of the tunnel that requires a flashlight and the outside noises begin to sound muffled. Swallowed by darkness, we continued to walk through the ongoing tunnel. Looking at our surroundings, there were tons of graffiti art and oddly-shaped concrete epoxy figures that sometimes looked like animals, objects, and other weird figures that accompanied us all throughout this tunnel. There also were some living animals that were in this tunnel as well. We had to watch where our head was because above us were sleeping bats. Cozied up in the natural holes from the tunnel, these nocturnal critters were scattered all along the top of these tunnels. We then came across the part of the tunnel where the diameter decreased by about a foot at around the 250-

yard checkpoint. Now we had no room above our heads, maybe an inch or two. This section was the largest part of the tunnel. Finally, the ending of this massive tunnel led to the waterfall room consisting of a few smaller tunnels and the roof is about 12 feet high. This sounds like a Stephen King movie, but I promise this is completely non-fiction. You can hear this waterfall flowing and dripping from almost the beginning of this whole tunnel. This area where the waterfalls are is so unique, with three small tunnels on one side and a metal ladder that leads up to another small tunnel on the other. The one small tunnel that was accessible by this ladder up to a drain that was below a street grate. We would sometimes sit under the grate and watch the cars drive over it, echoing the loud tire noises throughout the tunnels. Once we began to make frequent trips to the waterfall room, the three tunnels on the side prompted more curiosity. The only main issue was that the three tunnels were just big enough to crawl through.

We had explored the main tunnel, but the small tunnels were still a mystery. With curiosity fueling the fire, it was the same procedure as the first time exploring the tunnels. Gather resources, allow enough time to get to the unknown destination, and make it back. The only difference was, we would be on our hands and knees the whole way through. Nothing but crawling for hours it seemed. We couldn't stand up and stretch, couldn't just get up and walk out, it was definitely a commitment. A commitment to exploration. Taking breaks for snacks and regaining stamina was a more common occurrence than usual. This might've been a hair shorter or just as long as the final section of the main tunnel. The best feeling after reaching the end of this painful journey was seeing the light of another street grate above this drain tunnel. We crawled the remainder of the way and were able to stand up and gaze upon the new world we had come upon like a scene in *Narnia*. It was an entirely new neighborhood from which we had come from. I still have no reference to how far that was or where that destination is. All I know is we had done what we had set out to achieve.

The city would do on and off construction by the tunnels and that gave us a great opportunity to climb on anything we could and pretend we were operating the construction equipment. There was one point during the construction process where they had built up a humongous dirt pile, about 35 feet tall and about 40 feet wide. We would make our way up the pile then jump out and as far as we could go into the dirt below. This was such an amusing thing to do because we could jump from something so high up and it didn't hurt at all because we landed in several feet of soft non-compacted dirt. There was one time where we had the brilliant idea of getting Ben's toy Batman wings to act as a makeshift hang glider and seeing if we could get lift-off at the top. We took turns swapping the Batman wings, riding the small wave of hope we had that we would become the next Wright Brothers from this dirt pile.

After countless hours no one successfully achieved flight, what a shocker.

During winter, while the construction equipment was out, we would pretend we were in a Star Wars movie, walking across an icy lake with heavy machinery nearby. Wielding imaginary lightsabers and hopping in machine after machine and imagining we were the top-tier X-Wing pilots saving the galaxy. The wintertime was a period where we could experience all the aspects of this weather in a creek environment. We were so amazed with how thick the ice got in some areas and would make it a yearly tradition to dedicate a day to break up all the ice. The winter also served as a tough learning experience. As much fun as we had playing in the snow, the ice was an underlying threat. With water being present in the creek 80% of the time, that made the majority of the concrete extremely slippery, you can probably see where this is going. Over by the cliff area, it got extremely slippery, the combination of ice and frozen moss, made it the perfect way to get hurt if you weren't careful. One day Ben and I were playing around by the cliff. At times I would carefully stand on the edge and sometimes slide my feet, always intrigued by the impending doom that was possible from this cliff. As I walked around on the top, I happened to step on an especially slippery part of the concrete. I immediately felt my feet come up from underneath and I knew what was next. I fell right on my back and to make things better, I somehow got momentum from the initial fall and began to slide off the edge. How could I have possibly put myself in this position? Falling in the air I remember thinking this was the worst possible thing to happen. All the times we said "man that would hurt if you fell from there," well here I was doing it. I hit the ground with what felt like the force of a thousand planets crashing down. It's a weird feeling falling from a high place and time feels still. Once I came to, I knew I wasn't dead or seriously injured, so I checked that off the list. Ben obviously saw my graceful fall to the bottom and asked if I was okay. I felt incredibly sore, not taking into account if I had broken anything or not. I headed home soon after, sore, defeated, but soon to return.

Ben and I found out about a video uploading site called YouTube and we were already interested in playing out war scenes with toy guns and coming up with all this crazy stuff, therefore we thought why not record and produce short films to upload to YouTube. We started out filming short Lego videos with his mom's camcorder, then once we got iPod touches, we began filming with those. We transitioned from aimlessly playing in the creek and having occasional Nerf battles to sitting down and thinking about how we could turn it into something with a storyline or a small plot for a short film. We would sit in Ben's room and go back and forth, sharing video ideas and see which one sounded the best. It was like we were young directors in the making; Every week it seemed we were filming all sorts of war battles and fight-to-the-death short films. At the time, the show *The Walking Dead* was blowing up in popularity, and Ben and I got the great influence to integrate zombies and fight off the undead in our war films. I had seen tons of zombie Nerf wars on YouTube that made us want to make our own. We made numerous video series of this style of videos, having our siblings and friends play different roles. We gradually got better at editing and visual effects, by downloading VFX apps on our iPods and editing these crazy props into the videos like muzzle flashes, giant explosions, and car crashes. This helped take our creativity to the next level of video editing and encouraged us to create more videos.

We also hung out with a kid named Thomas, who was the Grandson of the folks who lived next to Ben. The times that Thomas was visiting, he would hang out with Ben and I. After hanging out a whole bunch, we eventually established a small fictional city in our neighborhood called "NickTomBen" or "NTB." It was our own little town with government positions and assigned land. It consisted of the storm drain, the creek, and all of our different tree forts in our backyards. The fort in my backyard was small, but it kept me entertained fairly well and served as the perfect candidate for our newly found town headquarters. I named the fort "The Black Bombers." I'm not sure why I chose to name my fort this, but it sounded cool and it gave me a great sense of possession. One day I hopped up on the railing, hanging on the side with one arm as I wrote the name in light blue chalk with my fourth grade handwriting. Since that day, I didn't touch that drawing until years to come. Ben's fort was smaller than mine but connected to this tree that had places to sit on, which inevitably made it a great meeting spot. Thomas didn't have a fort, though he had this plastic play set on the balcony in his backyard that ultimately became our marketplace center.

Expanding my fort was easily my favorite part of being a citizen of our town. It was like having a castle in a kingdom and I wasn't going to settle with a mediocre, boring one. Finding wood from trash piles, scavenging leftovers from my dad's projects, contributed to the funding of my infrastructure. This is what started my passion and enjoyment of building things with my hands and figuring out how small scale structural integrity behaved. Wood, nails, and a hammer; the holy trifecta that were the fundamentals of my castle.

When Thomas was in town, we would dedicate days to explore different areas to hypothetically claim as our land to add to the town. The Oklahoma Land Run event at school taught us well in this scenario. Backyard after backyard we would walk through and just enjoy the experience of being somewhere we probably weren't supposed to be. It was easy to do this because, on the one side of the creek, it connected to everyone's backyard with no fencing. The no fencing aspect was a blessing and a curse because even though we could travel with no barriers, so could a crazy aggressive dog that lived nearby. On days we would explore, we would sometimes come across this dog that was allowed to roam behind this house with no fence. This dog happened to have quite the temper, one good look at you and it was in your best interest to start running. We also created landmarks of people's decor in their backyards such as statues, fake water wells, and old sheds. Before we knew it we had expanded on our town, like we were unofficial rulers of the neighborhood.

The three of us would be playing down by the creek and sometimes we would come across other kids that were slightly older than us, hanging out down there as well. One aspect of being around kids who are older than you is that there are times where you either try to prove you're on their level to not get looked down on or submit to the fact that the older kids will always be superior. Growing up, I never liked to purposely mess with kids that were younger than me, but there are plenty of other people that feed off that power. There was this group of neighborhood kids that went to our school and the times we came across them in the creek they would give us dirty looks like they didn't like us or we were impeding on their socializing. When they would say something to us I had no problem saying something witty back and sometimes Ben or Thomas would add something in to get their word out. Throughout my life, I was building the ability to let people know that they couldn't push me around. There was one person who stuck out to me in this group who I truly hated. To be clear they all were not nice to us, but this guy would sometimes randomly say some smart comments to us to show off to his friends and he had this attitude like there was no one was above him. Even though they were older, I always had the thought that if I had to throw down, I would give it my all and hope for the best.

There came a day where we came across this group again and it started with typical banter similar to "Well well, you guys again." The back and forth talk went on, and it seemed like one of the kids subtly picked up a small rock and threw it our way. Me having the mindset of what someone did to me, I would do it right back. I may have been the first of us to return fire, but I'm not too clear on who exactly threw a rock back. Either way, we were not afraid of putting up with these guys. In a flash, it turned into a dodgeball fight with rocks. I was scrambling looking on the ground, trying to find the best rocks that could be thrown and do some damage. Most of the rocks thrown by both parties were missed. Bobbing and weaving, we landed a few on them and we got hit as well. One piece of this story that I'll never forget, is that the same kid that I hated the most out of the group, struck me with a solid throw. As this rock fight was going on, I fixated on him picking a rock up like it was slow motion in a movie. I was focused on nothing but seeing him pick up this rock frame-by-frame. I saw his eyes look up and lock on me. He lifted his arm and launched that rock like he was being drafted in the MLB. This was an absolute missile of a throw that had this rock coming right towards me. It was a sudden hit with a strong impact as it struck me right above my left eye. Immediately this put me in the state of getting the heck out there! I turned my shoulders and began sprinting off of the hill we were on. I knew I didn't get hit lightly just by the way it felt. Thomas and Ben followed soon after they saw I got popped in the face. I was on a mission of running straight back to the house and not looking back. I came to the house crying and holding my head, as my mom took a look at me and a giant goose egg had formed. For months I had a little bump from that same spot where I got hit. Thomas, Ben, and I referred to that incident as "The Great Rock Fight" past that point, from what I can remember, we never saw them again.

It's interesting thinking about all the stuff I did with a few friends when I was that age. Mario kart, Nerf guns, the creek, all of it was awesome. Definitely happy to say I don't think my childhood was boring in that sense, nor do I think Ben's parents or my parents knew just how much we explored those tunnels. Either way it makes for great storytelling and a few life lessons sprinkled in there. My life would probably be so different If I weren't able to go outside and explore. My advice would be to let your kids explore at a young age, there's only so much to do depending where they grow up and those small experiences can hold onto them throughout their lives.

3

A Bond with the Board

Who knew how much I would grow to love a piece of wood with four wheels. I guess you could say I had always liked extreme sports whether it was BMX, Motocross, or Snowboarding. Though one stuck out like it was my calling to pursue, that was skateboarding. I had seen a few books with Tony Hawk and other famous skateboarders on them, but I never ever thought about actually getting into it. I was riding the bus in about the first grade and saw this kid outside my window on a skateboard. I thought that's the sport that I saw in that book. He then did an ollie, which blew my mind at the time thinking you can move your feet in a way that lifts the board up in the air with you, without moving it by hand. I sat there and told myself that I would be able to do that one day because it looked so cool. I got on my dad's old computer and began swimming in the vast ocean of old Tony Hawk videos and 90's skate part videos with Rodney Mullen, Daewon Song, Chris Cole, and many more. I sat there and dreamed what life would be like if I were to become just as good as them. I didn't fully realize it at the time, but I believe the real reason I like skateboarding is that there are infinite variations of making a plank of wood move, unlike any other sport. Skateboarding just seemed to be the most complex and interesting sport to get into and I had this burning fascination about the athletics behind the sport and how talented you had to be in order to do this. I never had any friends that were interested in skateboarding at the time, but I took it upon myself to learn and discover everything about this sport.

I had brought up to my parents that I was interested in this and maybe wanted to buy a board in an attempt to begin learning. They told me it was a dangerous sport and the likelihood of getting hurt was near certain. They probably were also hesitant on the idea because skateboarders have a reputation of defiance and recklessness, and they might've thought that I would turn into the cliche image of a skateboarder one day. Surprisingly my grandmother was more open to the idea of getting me a skateboard and then it became more of a reality of chasing this passion. Sometime around the age of six, my grandmother and I went to a sports and outdoor store, where I browsed the skateboard section. I was so unfamiliar with skateboards, brands, and how they were made. All I knew is that I was looking for a round rectangular shape of wood and four wheels that looked cool. To no surprise, I was the biggest fan of the cartoon show, SpongeBob SquarePants. Once I saw that his face was on a skateboard, no other options seemed valid. Once we returned to my grandmother's house, I immediately took the plastics off while admiring that this was the beginning of something I knew I would love.

Stepping on a skateboard for the first time is like stepping on a small sheet of ice in the middle of an ocean. The board will move one way or another, regardless if you think it will cater to your movements. I had never heard quotes relating to getting better at a sport like: "practice makes perfect" or "Keep trying and you'll eventually get better" It was a true blind leap into this hobby, with not a clue if I was going to get better at skateboarding or not. Almost every day after school, I would skate around in my driveway, up and down the street, trying to get more comfortable with how a skateboard moves. I was unintentionally getting my body intertwined with the flow of movements needed for skateboarding. Each pebble I went over, each patch of pavement, added more and more to my ability to adjust while standing on a board. Years went by and I began to learn beginner tricks, such as Ollies, kick turns, carving, and manuals. Even though this period took years of practice, I realized if I had been more immersed in this sport, my learning process would've been catapulted. My dad had pointed out there was this skate park a few towns over from us that I might be interested in going to. I was so excited to be able to skate on an actual skatepark. My parents would take me multiple times a week here so I could continue to get better. I got to see all sorts of people at this skatepark, from innocent kids who went to the local school to older drug addict kids that used this skatepark to avoid facing problems at their work or within themselves. This was another eye-opener to what some people's lives are like, other than people I went to school with. I went to this skatepark a lot growing up because there were always challenges to work up to and I had become friends with a few people that visited there often. It was also the first time where I saw people in person that were tremendously better than me. Asking them for advice and tips for the tricks I was working on at the time was a big factor in my progression. I'm appreciative of the time it's taken to have an intimate learning experience and understand more deeply about this sport. Countless videos on trick tutorials and tips benefited me greatly on this journey. Trial and error is the absolute best principle behind this sport because you have no idea how exactly the board will move based on your body movements. You just have to see for yourself what exact muscle movements will get the board to do what you want.

Skateboarding in some way is like a teacher. It will literally throw you down until you get back up and figure out how to do it better. It is a constant unforgiving learning process that kept me interested because the skill had to be earned through perseverance and consistency. I couldn't tell you all the times where I sat there looking at my board in frustration and anger thinking why isn't this working? I'm doing all I can to try to learn this! Then after collecting my thoughts, I always come back around to the idea that

I just have to keep trying different things and eventually I'll get it down, that statement is 100% true in every sense. What also kept me interested in skateboarding is the reward factor of learning new tricks. It's an unbelievable feeling of accomplishment when you've been doing nothing but failing at something for months, then one day, one moment, you succeed. The simple cycle of failure and success drives this sport.

Skateboarding has also led me to crazy places and meeting even crazier people. Since I prefer the style of street skating, it promotes the idea of using the environment around you to see what's possible to do tricks off of. Anywhere I go with my board, I look at the infrastructure of places and imagine what I could do to come up with skating on the structures. Almost every time I would visit my grandma's house, I would dedicate time to skate at this church that was down the street. The pavement was smooth and there were numerous obstacles that were skateable, making it perfect for what I needed. I had skated outside this church tons of times and never came across anyone, but there was a time where someone approached me offering something they wouldn't offer to the police. I was there skating and I noticed two guys walking on the sidewalk that were significantly older than me, probably around 18 or 20. The initial concern was they both were looking at me like they were going to approach me. Sure enough, one of them split off from the other and walked towards me

"Hey, you're Zack right?" He said.

"No," I replied. He looked at me kind of funny like I was lying to him. He then goes "Are you sure you're not Zack? Because you look a lot like him." 11-year-old me was petrified at this point. I didn't know if this Zack person had made this guy mad or Zack owed this guy something and here I am caught in the middle of a misunderstanding.

"No, my name's Nick and I don't know who Zack is."

He then looks down and pulls out a bag while saying "Oh okay, well he was supposed to buy this from me."

I looked at the bag he pulled out of his pocket confused as to why this guy had a bunch of dried-up broccoli in this dirty bag of his.

"Do you want some?"

"No, I'm alright."

"Alright well see ya later man." He caught up with his friend and a wave of relief crashed over me once I realized I didn't get shot or robbed. I've never skated so fast back to the house in my life to get away from whatever just happened. I told my family about it and that's when it was later explained that he was offering me weed. It was ironic after our school had told us this might be a possible scenario in our life and you never think it'll happen to you, but sure enough, it can.

When I was about 12 years old I heard that one of the local skateparks was having a skate contest. I was intrigued because I was quite young and got consistent with some of the beginner to intermediate tricks. I thought you know what, I might as well shoot my shot and see how good I can do. I had my mom drive me up to the skatepark and I skated over to the booth. I poorly wrote my name in the small rectangle box given and I was signed up for the competition. I found out there is a bracket system in the contest where there were beginners, intermediate, and advanced. I signed up in the intermediate division because I wasn't adequately skilled, but I felt like I could keep up in intermediate. I only knew some of the harder basic tricks but I knew how to do them consistently. The announcer gave a quick speech and the contest was on. The beginners went first and then came intermediate, my heart started racing. I was stuck thinking I've never done this before and it was exciting being surrounded by people that were way better than me, as well as people that were worse. That's the type of middle ground I was in that made me feel satisfied. The intermediate class rolled around and I was the third to go in my division. After the first two guys went, I thought I had it in the bag. I got out my iPod and played the song "6 God" by Drake, it was my hype song at the time. I tried my hardest and did a couple of tricks that I felt were solid enough for my division, a few kickflips, a trick on the quarter pipe, and ended with a backside 50-50 grind with a shuv-it out. Throughout the run, I felt pretty confident knowing the results by the end. After the competition, we all got to gather around the announcement stand where the guy would announce the results. The beginners got all their results and prizes, then the intermediate division was next, which I was super anxious for. It went off a point system on the way they categorized the difficulty in my run to then determine my overall score. I thought I didn't do that great of a run, but it turns out I got second place in my division, which I was pleased with. I got a few stickers and a pat on the back. It was a cool experience for me to go there and see what's beyond skateboarding, competition-wise. It also gave me a future reference for the next time I wanted to enter a competition.

Later in Intermediate School, I met a few guys who also shared an interest in skateboarding. We would go out after school, load up on snacks and drinks at the nearest corner store, and skate all these places around town. While we were skating at these spots, we would often talk about what's going on at school, music, and overall just enjoying our time as we tried to land cool tricks wherever we were at. One aspect that stuck out to me during this time was that I could tell which person loved skateboarding or whether they were just doing it because their friends did. I didn't care what the reason was behind them wanting to skate because it was nice to share that commonality with people my age.

I did get a bit of criticism for being a part of a sport that is infamous for mischievous behavior, such as vandalism and drug use, in which neither of those I participate in. This was why when people asked what I liked to do, I would always mention skateboarding last. Now I have no shame in saying that I skate because I'm older and I know within myself why I do. A lot of people that I came across did not understand the idea to not judge a book by its cover. There would be times where me or my friends would be skating outside these businesses and some person would come out in anger, yelling at us saying to leave, or threaten to call the police. The one disconnect to this situation is that it's hard to explain to junior high kids why they don't want us there. It's always "Get out, you're destroying the property!" and not "Can you please leave, because if you get hurt we do not want to be held responsible for your injuries." We rarely came across kind, respectful, and understanding adults who politely told us to leave, but they're out there. In my view, it's a lot easier for people to yell and get angry than to try to clearly communicate their reasoning to get their point across. This confrontational approach never worked for the people using it. My friends and I were quick to state why we should be able to stay there regardless of us making them upset. They didn't get our reasoning in the sense that we saw it as a place to enjoy our hobby, like painting art by a pond or playing Frisbee in open land. It's only until I got older, I realized the proper ways of where to skate and why people don't want you skating on their land.

I eventually kept getting better and better, at this sport I was not losing interest in skateboarding after many years. I began to realize I was drastically better than anyone my age at my school. Some kids were star soccer players, others were flawless at math, and I happened to be pretty decent on a skateboard. Every single day, month, year, I was pushing myself to get better than anyone I knew. I then began to learn about sponsorships and how skateboarding companies will hire you to represent their brand by sending you clothes, skateboards, and a whole bunch of stuff. How this used to work was you would send them your best footage of you skating and they would get back to you on whether it looked like you had what it took to be a part of their company. Kind of like a physical copy of a resume for skateboarding. I thought that it would be such a life-changing idea if I ever came close to the opportunity of being affiliated with these huge name-brand skate companies. After watching the legendary movie *Street Dreams* and my skate friends telling me more about sponsorships, it was only a matter of time before I gave it a shot.

After months of collecting about an hour's worth of footage and trying to get my hardest tricks on film, I Eventually compiled my best clips to put in the video I was going to send out. In the summer of 2015, I sent out my five-minute video to all the name-brand skate companies I could. I followed the instructions of how to send them a "Sponsor Me" tape and crossed my fingers. I knew I wasn't as good as someone older than me, but it was worth a try, right? I sat there looking at my email inbox for days, anticipating that "Welcome to the Team!" reply. The majority of the brands I sent my video to did not reply, but surprisingly I had a few that wrote me back with a nice response. Most of them were along the lines of "Hey dude we loved your video, keep it up! Unfortunately, there's not a spot on the team right now, but we appreciate you sending the video to us." I knew that was probably a code word for I wasn't good enough, but I digress.

After more years of skating, I eventually hit this plateau of skill. There's a common experience among skaters, where one becomes consistent at intermediate and advanced level tricks, and it's difficult to get better. I began to realize that skateboarding to me should remain a form of relaxation and not something I should turn into a career. A skateboard has always seen me on my best days and on my worst days. It always seems to clear my head and help me overcome day-to-day problems. It makes me think about nothing but what's happening under my feet, and I want to keep it that way.

4

Land of the Learning

3 ...2...1...RING! Thank the lord for that bell going off or I would've been stuck there forever! Let me introduce to you my thought process during primary school. I had no idea what the meaning of anything was. When I went to school, I didn't question anything and went about my days, but some days packed more excitement than others. I was nothing short of a gremlin in the classroom and honestly, I don't think it was me purposely being defiant, it was just how I thought at the time. I almost had more days sitting in the principal's office than I did in the classroom up until about sixth grade. I never saw it as I was such a bad kid because there were kids doing way worse things than what I was getting in trouble for! Teachers never gave me a good enough reason to make me change what I was doing, nor would I ever listen to a loud, snappy, and unconstructive person. Half of my teachers barely had their lives together and here they were attempting to correct mine. Parent-teacher conferences were a

joke, my counselors couldn't find the right answers, but thankfully my parents knew where I was coming from in most situations and did what they could to help.

I was always getting messed with at school; and when it was my turn to retaliate, the teacher would turn around and boom, off the principals once again. I was an easy target for bullies, small hands, young for my grade, and my last name happens to sound the same as hamburger. I even got held back in the 2nd grade because all my peers were substantially older than me and my parents wanted me to be the same age as everyone, that definitely didn't make things any better. Others would just pick on me for the sake of picking on me. There was a kid named Josh, who was a fourth-grader when I was in about the first or second grade. One time we came across each other in the restroom. He mouthed out something hurtful, but I tried to ignore it. He didn't like that I had no reaction, so he held me by my neck up against the outside of a stall door and began to tell me how worthless I was and a whole bunch of mean things. Then after he released me and left, I couldn't believe what just happened and that moment has always stuck out when I think about the people that have messed with me. Let's take a quick snapshot of a funny story in the early days of kindergarten. They were this girl and we'll call her Faith for this story. Faith was no stranger to the practice of teasing me. One evening in Fall, my class and I were walking back inside from recess, and for no particular reason, Faith decided she wanted to make fun of me for my polar bear hat I was wearing. My grandparents got this hat from Alaska and I wore it all the time. On and on she went about how silly my hat looked, this and that. This was one of the first times in my life where I stood up for myself. Without hesitation, I turned around and pushed Faith down on the concrete path...right outside of the head principles window. This was the first patch of snow that snowballed these common occurrences of getting caught at the wrong time for something I didn't initiate. Other times I got myself in trouble because I was naive and I trusted others before knowing what things meant. An example of this was around third grade when I was sitting in timeout. For whatever reason, I was in timeout with another kid I was decently friends with. I was not up to date on the latest offensive slang terms used to make people mad, but my friend sure was. Sitting across from me at the timeout table at recess he looks up and says

"Hey Nick, hold up your hand."

Going along with him, I held up my hand.

"Now put down your thumb, pointer finger, ring finger, and pinky."

He starts laughing hysterically as I'm sitting here confused about what type of magic trick I thought he had me do. His laughing was suddenly cut short by our yelling teacher looking over and seeing my rude hand gesture. Quite flustered that I had been set up by my peer, right in front of our teacher, and back to the principals I went to.

There was some point in my school life where I began to use violence rather than coming to an agreement of differences. I was never the one to throw the first punch, but I would always make sure to have the last. Sometimes you can't solve your bullies with just your words and school was the only place to settle it. I got in a good amount of fist-to-fist situations, some I won and some I definitely lost. I felt like the kids who were rude and went out of their way to make kids feel bad needed some repercussions. I was at recess one day in middle school and there was a kid who I had often had problems with prior to this, but there was no given opportunity to have some time in the ring. We started arguing about something or he was bothering me in some way and tensions began to rise. He had a bad temper and sometimes I think that his dad might've been an aiding factor in his behavior. Bantering back and forth and being as explicit as a middle schooler can be. I must've said something that made that bright blonde mohawk of his stand up straighter than the hair of a porcupine because it was in an instant, the gloves were on. Trading punches, we went back and forth in the middle of this playground. I had to make sure to give it my all during fights, especially if there were other people around to show I could hold my own. At one point he went for a grapple of some sort and I went to shove him off. In the process of him falling, he grabbed my arrowhead chain that was from a deceased grandfather and ripped it off my neck. I felt completely destroyed. He already disrespected me and now he had indirectly disrespected my grandfather. I could feel the charging rage after the moment the chain left my neck and fell into the wood chips. I now threw my punches like I was the embodiment of Spartacus. Sooner or later, our friends ran over and pulled us apart. I still remember the look he had after the fight, beet-red face, and his mohawk no longer looked like a mohawk.

There was an episode on *Drake and Josh* where Drake was talking to Josh about not always having to follow the rules and he said "When people play dirty, sometimes you have to play dirty back" and I translated that thought process to when these kids would push things a little too far. It came to a point where I felt like I had to prove that I could defend myself or they would continue to mess with me. There were plenty of kids that talked a lot of trash and had messed up lives at home, but I don't think that was an excuse to carry that character onto other people.

There was even one fight where a boiling rival of mine wrote on my face and shirt with a black expo marker on the bus. I then grabbed the marker from his hand and quickly took my Picasso skills to his shirt. We happened to get off at the same stop and as I stepped off the bus, I turned around to see how this would escalate. Sure enough, I got a sucker-punched dead center in the face. Stunned but not down, we threw our backpacks down by the stop sign and started swinging like two intoxicated monkeys. I won't deny, he was one of the better opponents for his size. The grappling, accuracy of his punches, dodging, it was all impressive. He then spun around, jumped on my back, and put me in a headlock that almost took me to the ground. I then flipped him clear over my shoulders and started landing shots on the back of his head. The producers over at WWE would've given me a contract and a healthy pension after seeing that move. The young man bus driver hopped out and ran over to us, somewhat easily separating us. We both split ways and I walked home with an increasingly swelling hand. Later that evening at the local urgent care, we find out that my hand is indeed broken. In a cast and unfortunately out for the remainder of my football season. It was a pain in the butt having to write things in school because it was my left hand, I learned to write with my right hand during the time of my cast. Though this wasn't the last time I'd get into an altercation on the bus. There was this guy I hated on my football team, granted there were several guys I didn't like, but I had always butted heads with this one previous to football. While riding on the bus, he starts making fun of my friend who was a little on the bigger side. Calling him fat and saying he eats too much; obviously, I'm not going to sit there and do nothing, hence I told him to knock it off. He then turned back around in his seat and continued to shame my friend. He happened to have a swollen and infected finger that caught my eye every time he put his hands on the top of the seat. I saw that as his weak point I could use to get him to shut up. Once

I saw the opportunity, I hammer fisted directly onto that finger, it was like real-life Whac-A-Mole. I had now rattled the beehive. He calmly stared up at me like I had just slapped his mom in front of him. Before I knew it, he shot off a solid punch to my chest that sent me falling into the middle of the bus aisle. He sat back down and no one said a word after that. A couple of years went by and I rarely got close to having to raise my hands ever again. Though I always thought during high school that a few guys needed the snot beat out of them, but we were older and I knew they would get what's coming. I have many more stories of my short-lived boxing career during school, but I only wanted to mention the juicy ones.

Having relationships in these early years of school always cracks me up thinking about what lengths we had to go to for our crush to notice us. At recess, we'd all be playing tag and if you weren't the fastest one out there, no valentine's day card for you. There was a time in elementary school where I thought I was going to marry this girl named Aubrey, but when I got held back in the 2nd grade, it felt like my chances of that were shot down. I remember how competitive it was back in middle school as well, to date a cute girl for no other reason than to say you all were dating. If a girl would give a guy a pack of colored pencil grips or any number of Silly Bandz, it was a sure sign she liked him. I remember being at the lunch table with a few friends, sometime in the fifth grade, and we noticed a girl glance over at us for less than 3 seconds and we'd all huddle closer and say things like

"I can't tell, did she look at you or did she look at me?"

"I'm pretty sure she was looking at me"

"No dude, her eyes were definitely pointed on my side of the table."

It was a battleground to say the least. I would get so jealous if one of my friends would happen to get a girlfriend one week and I would think, that could've been me! Though it always would save me the trouble of being around the wildfires of drama that comes with a circle of girls. Of course, it was always satisfying to see the relationships of others crumble because of the minor inconveniences that upset one or the other. At this age, you are also not smart enough to see potential dangers in the simplest of things. In my math class during the fifth grade, I was sitting in my chair playing with my eraser. It was a common practice among our age to take the huge rectangular pink erasers and poke holes in them with pencils like it was a bulletin board. I thought I was the only one who did this until I grew up and learned that most everyone did this. I think because of its satisfying nature to puncture the soft material over and over. This particular day, I wanted to see if I could squeeze my pencil through to the other side of the eraser. My eraser already looked like a shooting target so I felt like I wasn't losing much if this eraser didn't hold up to my experiments. I held the eraser in my right hand, the goal was to allow the pencil to have room on the other side when it went through. I was fully gripping my pencil, holding it steady as I forced it down into the eraser. I thought it was slowly going to emerge on the other side, but I was wrong. The small pink rectangle object gave way like a water dam splitting down the middle and the pencil came shooting down into my hand. I tried to release the force, but I couldn't react fast enough. The tip of this number 2 pencil had burrowed in my palm. It didn't hurt at all, I just thought whoops, that pencil slipped a little faster than I wanted. Pretty soon a small amount of blood started forming and I quickly covered it up until class was over. I got a little concerned about how deep how the pencil went, my first thought was to see the nurse and have her look at it. I was sitting there while she held my hand underneath a lamp as she dug around with a knife of some sort. There was clearly graphite in my hand and she was trying her best to get as much of it out. The operation was unsuccessful as I went home with still some of it in my hand. I told my parents what happened and they didn't think it would cause any harm and so I didn't worry about it from then on. Sure enough, I haven't had any problems relating to it and still to this day I can see I have a little piece of the pencil lead in my hand from that day.

This is also around the time I first started hearing about people smoking weed. I didn't know anything about it besides it was bad. Yes, this was a little before middle school when we heard about kids starting into this. Occasionally I would hear stories about kids getting caught with it in their locker or having it in their backpacks. A few times at recess I could smell it coming from one side of the field where the group of the bad kids always hung out. It was best to not say anything to a teacher because I sure didn't want to be targeted after getting them in trouble. Aside from illegal business practices, some of us came up with a more creative way of making money. Duck tape wallets became of my many business trades in the school environment. Popularity grew in "Do-it-Yourself" crafts and it became a booming business for those taking advantage of the craze. My friend Josh, who was a friend of mine through skateboarding, introduced me to the idea of hand-making duck tape wallets. He showed me a few of his, all the colors, designs, and the engineering behind them. "A buck 50 to buy and I resell it for $5" he told me. I could not believe how easy that sounded. I got as many colors of duck tape as I could from Walmart and began the process. He had shown me how to make the perfect wallet and to tweak the features to make every wallet unique. For a few weeks, that's all we focused on was making wallet after wallet and selling them to kids around school, and making a profit. More and more kids began to figure out how to make these wallets and it couldn't have been a better example of supply and demand. The demand was decreasing and the supply across our school was for sure increasing. I eventually lost the motivation for making the wallets. After the trend, I had tons of spare wallets that I had laying around and I was glad I had accumulated a decent amount of money for what it was.

Everyone seemed to be involved in some type of sport or activity. I had a couple years of soccer prior and I thought about playing football as my "After school activity." I thought I looked weird if I wasn't a part of any activity during school. I kept signing up for these art classes hoping that they would be easy, but all I got from them were harsh judgments of my work and even I had one art teacher directly tell me I looked exactly like her ex-husband...she had it out for me the rest of the year. The school system encouraged us to get into something even though we might've not wanted to. We had a musical instrument department with two paths you could enroll in for an elective/activity, that being band or orchestra. When I was 13 the word "band" meant drums, electric guitars, and a lot of pizza. Needless to say, after hearing that I could sign up for band class as an activity for school, I was all in. My expectations were shot down after I signed the enrollment card. I later found out the class is composed of these instruments: trumpet, trombone, saxophone, drums, French horn, flute, and the piccolo. After taking a look at the not-so-desired list, I figured I could shoot my shot for the drums. This seemed to be the only instrument close to what I was looking for. The way it worked was you would write down what you wanted to play, then you would be interviewed by the music teacher to see if you were the right fit for the instrument you had picked. During my interview, I had explained that the drums seemed like an instrument that I was interested in because I had watched the show,

Zeke and Luther, and they often rocked out on air guitars and drums. Then I had to sell my persuasion by saying I was also interested in learning the rhythm within drumming, which was partially true. She sat there and seemed to have been half-listening to what I was saying.

"You know what I think you would be good at?" She asked. "You need to play the clarinet, you have nice lips for it."

A small feeling of being dismissed soon transferred into open-mindedness; maybe this is something new I could try out. They gave me a clarinet to borrow, while I had to pay for the small changeable mouthpieces. During the school year, we were supposed to be consistently practicing pieces of music and recording our minutes on a practice sheet. About half of the class actually did the practice sheets because they either enjoyed it or their parents made them. I fell into the other half; where I practiced a little, but at the end of the day, I didn't like any of it. It's hard to make a person do something if they don't truly enjoy it. A redeeming quality to practicing was preparing for the chair test. The chair tests were a weekly assessment to see how well we had learned to play the piece of music and that decided where we sat in class. The people who sat at the front were usually consistent and you could tell that they had practiced. The skill level slope declined the further back the seating arrangement went. Almost for every chair test, I simply played it by memory and tried to mimic the sounds of others who played the pieces before me. To no surprise, for most of the year, I stayed steady in the back half of the class. I had a few friends who were extremely successful in landing a spot close to the front. For some reason that never motivated me to try any harder because I felt like it wasn't much of a reward for just being able to say you sit at the front of the class. One remarkable experience I got from this class was there was this girl who I had become friends with during the year, but I was timid and did not have the nerve to tell someone I liked them, especially if I thought they were significantly more attractive than me. She had bright shiny blonde hair, a likable personality, and beaming blue eyes that lit up the room. I also was intimidated by the fact that she could practically play the clarinet behind her back and dominate the chair test. Her name was Bre. I had this friend at the time who happened to be great friends with Bre and I may have mentioned a few times I had a crush on this girl in my band class. Her eyes lit up once she made the connection of who I had my crush on. She was the type of friend to get the food cooking as soon as the ingredients were mentioned.

I threw her a bunch of "Well maybe," "What if...," "I don't know...,"

"I'm going to ask her about this next time I see her!" She told me.

I was freaking out, but at the same time excited because I knew it was in the hands of fate to see if this would go well. A few days passed and my friend ran up to me all jumpy and said "Alright, well you guys are dating now!" It was a weird feeling. It was like telling someone I wanted a Lamborghini and then a couple of days later they show up at my house with the exact one I wanted with no work I had to do to get it. I just went along and accepted it. Me being the person wanting to do things legitimately, the next time I saw Bre, I mentioned the funny situation that our friend had put us in and I wanted to formally ask her out. Sixth grade me scored the cutest girl in my band class and it didn't matter if I was terrible at the clarinet, because in my eyes I was winning!

I believe my teacher sympathized with me because even though I neglected getting better at the clarinet, I got along with everyone and was respectful. She often pulled me aside and questioned why I was doing so poorly and failing to accurately record the practice sheets. At first, I made excuses to not make it sound bad or not hurt her feelings, though later I eventually expressed how I got little to no enjoyment playing the clarinet. There even was a time that looked really bad when we had our winter band concert that we had been practicing for months. The night of the concert, I realized that I had left my clarinet in my locker at school. In my teacher's eyes, it probably looked like I had purposely done that, but to this day I promise it was an honest mistake. Bre and I broke up during the second semester of the year and I had solidified with myself that I never wanted to play the clarinet again. I had learned a lot about people and how the school system operates up to this point, but what I didn't know was that coming up next would be more socially dividing than I could ever imagine.

5

You've Got a Friend in Me

The process of making new friends and getting to know people is one of the most fascinating aspects of life we can experience. I had to pick and choose friends because I never knew how they would act in about a week or two. Some of my craziest experiences growing up come from all the kids in my neighborhood which now make for some great stories. I also made a bunch of friends during school that would later become great companions that stick around in my life. I had become friends with a guy at school that had similar interests as me and he happened to live a couple of blocks away. I knew he always had an unusual way of life, but he was so confident and had this attitude that kind of intrigued me to stick around and see what his life was like. We hung out a few times at his house, where his parents were rarely present. We shared the hobby of skateboarding and BMX; we would set up ramps and obstacles in his driveway to skate on along with going down the steep hill by his house. I always noticed his neighbor had a great big professionally built halfpipe in their backyard and I always thought about asking about ringing their doorbell and see if they would let us skate it, but we never did. The more I hung out with him, the more I saw the darker sides of his life. Like I said, his parents were never there and out of all the times we hung out, I think I met his mom maybe once. He had a rough relationship with his siblings, especially the brother. Oftentimes when I was over they would get into some fairly heated arguments and exchange some words that you probably wouldn't want to say to your mom. My friend was the oldest of the two brothers, so in his eyes, he probably thought he could boss him around. We were hanging at his house after school one time and his little brother was messing with him. It then escalated a bit more to where they were starting to scream at each other, and I was kind of standing there not knowing what to do. My friend lunged at him, trying to grab him and the brother dashed off. They ran into the kitchen, as I'm right behind them, and the younger brother went behind the kitchen table. It was like watching a cat-and-mouse game in this house and I didn't know how it was going to end. In a standoff, with the kitchen table in between them, they continued screaming at each other. Pretty soon, my friend gives up on trying to chase him and looks around for something nearby to throw across the table. He picks up an empty long-neck beer bottle and chucks it at his brother with no hesitation. The brother was able to dodge the bottle and it shattered everywhere into the wall behind them. It was absolutely crazy what just happened, that was one moment where I thought I didn't know if I'm too safe here. The fight was eventually diffused and the day went on. One funny addition from hanging out with this kid is he was the one who introduced me to rap music. He had explained to me how he started listening to rap and he wanted to show me a song. I'll never forget the moment we got on his dad's old computer and he pulled up the song "Watch My Shoes" by Lil Wayne. I had to have been close to 11 or 12 and this song was so explicit for my age, that I couldn't comprehend any of it. It was definitely a change to the usual music I had listened to, but I was enjoying it at the moment.

Before middle school, I never paid too much attention to who I was friends with or what they meant to me. It was almost as simple as thinking if they were nice to me and they didn't eat crayons, they were my friend.

One interesting time when I was around 12, I was great friends with this kid from school. I hung out at his house a bunch during school and over the summer, one time I accidentally set off the house alarm by opening a window. He was fairly wealthy and made my house look like a ramshackle. One night I was supposed to come over and hang out. When my mom dropped me off, we noticed there was a substantial amount of cars outside the house. I couldn't figure out why until I was walking up the steps to his house and then I remembered, it was his sister's 18th birthday. I walked in and it was a full-on house party with strobe lights and loud music. The song "Like a G6" was playing while I stood by the front door and looked at all these taller kids walking by. Still to this day, I'm about 99% sure the parents were not there. At this same house, I went over to celebrate his birthday and he invited a bunch of friends over from a few different schools. One kid that I met at his birthday party was some punk football player that went to our rivalry school and he was shredded for a fifth grader. His first impression didn't make him shine and I was already annoyed with this guy after an hour. For some reason during the night, we were upstairs in the game room and this kid got out his football pads. He joked around about hitting my friend and I for fun. My friend must've avoided it somehow because I was in the position to get hit. I didn't want to volunteer to be a football practice dummy, but when there are two guys your age who are bigger than you, you don't have many options. I was at one side of the room and he was at the other, he full-on sprints at me and plows me over like I was nearing his team's endzone. Surprisingly this was not the first time I had been in this situation, I must've had a shirt that said "I love getting beat up" because this type of scenario seemed to happen too many times. He ran into me a few more times before I started to show signs of hurting, once they noticed this, they figured it would then be funny to see how hard of a punch I could take on the arm. At this point, I felt like I was being targeted because my so-called "friend" was allowing his friend to make up ways to hurt me. After like 10 minutes of getting my arm punched,

I told myself this was enough. I remember thinking I wanted to fight both of them so badly, but A: I had never fought two people at once, and B: I didn't want to fight in his house with his parents' home. In hindsight, I totally should have, I shouldn't have let them get away with that regardless if his parents were there. I was able to get away and protect myself in a closet, there I called my mom and told her she needed to pick me up as soon as possible. I was sick of being pushed around by these kids another minute. Soon after, they started taunting me and calling me names outside of the closet door. I was no stranger to being called a number of names so they weren't making much ground. Once I got the text that my mom was there, I burst out that closest and ran out of the room, downstairs, and out of the house. I could care less about saying goodbye to the parents and who else was there, I knew I just had to get out of there. After that day, I never went back to his house again.

Towards the end of sixth grade, I noticed that a new kid came to our school and his class happened to be next door to mine. Though some things stuck out to me that made me want to get to know him. He often wore a Birdhouse Tony Hawk shirt and a pair of Vans slip-on shoes, which stood out because most everyone in our grade wore Nike, Adidas, Vera Bradley, Oakley lanyards, and a lot of neon. I don't recall exactly how we met, but at some point, I was able to mention to him that I was a fan of his clothes and I asked if he skated or not. He said he liked to ride his penny board and also mentioned he enjoyed making YouTube videos, which coincidentally, I was starting to get more into YouTube and making short films. I now met my new friend, Jonathan or Jon as he goes by. We hit it off great, sharing our similar passions and hobbies and getting to know each other during school. I came to find out that he lived in the same neighborhood as me, which made it convenient for when we wanted to hang out. He's super creative and open-minded to whatever there is to talk about and I could tell he was going to turn into a great friend of mine.

The transition into the Jungle of middle school was the next step in my journey. I had this underlying fear that I would be the last person for their voice to get deeper, but it turned out to be the opposite. The summer going into seventh grade, I was one of the first people for their voice to change. This was a double-edged sword because it was cool to show people you were getting this new voice, but a little awkward because you held the title of the black sheep until more people caught up for it to become "normal." My voice got significantly deeper in a short amount of time. I didn't experience a long period where my voice was cracking or slipping pitches a whole bunch. My family and I joke about how it almost happened overnight. Middle school was no doubt my biggest feat yet and I had no clue what to expect. I would say this was the point where everyone started to form cliques and social groups. For a long time, I tried to fit in fairly hard with the popular group of kids at our school. I would try to wear the same clothes, act like I was interested in the same things, talk like I had all these things when in reality I definitely didn't. I even remember telling this kid throughout the whole year I had an elevator in my house and he couldn't come see it because it "keeps breaking all the time." There was almost even a certain lingo I had to follow to not make me sound different from the popular kids. Life seemed better for them as they had all these friends they could rely on. It was this mindset that if I wanted to have a life like theirs, I would have to act a certain way to be considered "cool" and be accepted.

After being friends with Jon for a few months he introduced me to an old friend of mine, Truman. I had initially met Truman five years prior and we had become friends through Star Wars and Legos. Truman is one of the most exceptionally unique friends I have and I've learned so much from his great storytelling and perseverance. It's worth mentioning when he was nine he was diagnosed with a rare form of bone cancer called Osteosarcoma and lost his right leg in sacrifice for his life. Thankfully he recovered and returned back to our school. He had become friends with a group of guys and I was getting into video games, which put me in with a different friend group. This kept us from crossing paths for a few years. It was ironic when Jon wanted to introduce me to him because I already knew him quite well. Nonetheless, I was excited that Jon was becoming friends with Truman. Jon and I hung out a bunch outside of school. Our mutual enjoyment for Youtube brought us together in the sense of sharing future ideas and what videos we liked to film. After I told him all the experience I had filming videos with Ben and having a ton of fun with that, it was only a matter of time until we began filming our own short films. Jon definitely played more of the director role and loved coming up with comedy skit ideas to film. We would meet up at our local playground and talk for hours about what life would be like if we were to pursue filmmaking as a career, or expanding YouTube into a job. We eventually made a YouTube channel with both of us called "NickAndJonTV." For weeks we consistently made these short skits to upload to this channel, one of the first skits we made was called "Body Building Fail." It was where our main character, Mike Bufferson, was played by Jon and he was training my character on how to get buff, by doing all these exercises and athletics. It was based on the movie style of Rocky and Jon edited in copyright-free music of a remake of the song "Eye of the Tiger." Jon and I rode the same bus from about sixth grade until high school, on that bus we met two girls that we made friends with, Julie and Caroline. I met Julie first and ironically enough, I used to skate with her older brother years ago and he was a great guy so I figured Julie was nice as well. Julie also happened to live in our neighborhood and she would come to meet Truman and begin hanging out with all of us. Caroline was her friend and when I tell you I don't think I've met a kinder and sweeter soul than hers, I'm not kidding. I couldn't get enough talking to Caroline for the simple fact that she brought peace to a conversation. I appreciate that in people because it was hard to have practical conversations with people our age and many of them could not get over their ignorance.

During the summer going into middle school, there was a local soccer event going on for kids that went to our school district. It was there on the dirt field, where I met another one of my long-term friends, Jackson. I then later introduced Jackson to Jon and Truman at the lunch table at school. We all became inseparable friends after a short time. We often went to the movie theatre, went to the skatepark, hung out at each other's house, and our friendship was only going to get better. At some point, we wanted to have some sort of group name, a label that defined our friend group. One day Truman, Jon, and I were at a skatepark and I had randomly come up with the name "The Hot Sauce Pack" or THSP for short. The name really had no meaning, but it sounded fitting and the name stuck.

That next semester, Jon and I signed up to be in our school's news broadcasting program called "Trojan Broadcasting System" or TBS, as most people called it. This was a completely different environment of the school, no assignments, no due dates, and we got to use real camera equipment? Heck yes! This was a perfect opportunity for Jon and I, since we had already had so much experience with cameras. Jackson joined us soon after because this piqued his interest as well. Since we were in the younger grade, we had access to a few things and basically were bird watchers in this class the rest of seventh grade. A few months later I then met Andrew and Skylar, both were great guys I met in school and they eventually became a part of our group. This to me was the first friend group that I cared about, they all were different from the usual people I talked to. They had similar hobbies and ways of thinking that made them important people in my life. I would play Xbox for hours with Skylar and Andrew happened to go to Jackson's church.

Jackson had mentioned there was an annual color war hosted by their church that was coming up soon and wanted the whole Hot Sauce Pack to join. Word got around to the rest of the group and pretty soon we had a color war on the schedule! This color war was basically hundreds of kids that had bags of colored powder and there were buckets scattered around the field that kids could grab more powder from. It was also ideal to wear a white T-shirt so the colors would show up better. All six of us were on board with this and ready to go. It was August of 2014, we all met up at Jackson's church and were ready for battle. I had my GoPro propped up on my head, trying to get footage for my Youtube channel. Every so often I go back and watch the video and I can still remember the feeling of being there. About 75 degrees, the sun was about to go down, and there was a smell of a distant grass fire. There were tons of kids. I was honestly overwhelmed with how many different age groups there were on this 10-acre field. It was a sea of white T-shirts as we made our way to the stage that was on one side of the field. The church band was playing some rock music as a precursor to the war. We were jamming out to the band and getting all excited, ready for this event. The lead singer gets a hold of the mic as the music is building he says

"I want to see all this color go so high that people driving down the highway stop and they're like, what is this color explosion and why am I not a part of it? I want you to go as crazy as you can and throw it as high as you can."

The music kept building and I could tell we were about to get wild.

He then says "Are you ready?! On my count, 3,2,1 go- NO NO NO!"

Everyone threw up their bags of color prematurely. It was hilarious; he made it sound like when he said "3,2,1 go" we were supposed to throw it, but I guess he was trying to let us know what he was going to say before we threw it. The band accepted that everyone threw their color bags and continued playing the rest of the song while color was going everywhere. Everyone then ran away from the stage and headed out into the field. This is when we locked and loaded on as much colored powder as we could hold. There were even socks being thrown with powder in them like they were Molotov cocktails. In a matter of seconds, all the air in this field was a big cloud of color. All these kids were running blindly through the smoke as I was trying to find where my friends went during the chaos. The event went on for a few hours, but the sun was almost completely down. We finally left after throwing the last of the powder left in those buckets. We took our crazy-looking shirts and headed to the nearest QuikTrip to end the night with some slushies. My first experience at a color war was one to remember

The second year of middle school was upon us, and I was ready for whatever was coming my way. This is the year where my life changed forever. In TBS we were all around the popular kids and star athletes, they ran the show and purposely would not talk to you if you weren't in their social group. The teacher who led TBS was none other than Mr. Ravenscroft, who also was the engineering teacher. He was the most unique, hilarious, and nontraditional teacher I had ever met in my life. There were rumors he had fake hair and had lost his eye in a sand storm in some other country, which added to his uniqueness. He was a straightforward, unforgiving, but sarcastic guy, who loved diet Coke. Everyone loved him because he was incomparable from the other teachers at our school and he gave kids credit on the jobs they could do as far as bettering the program. He would let the kids, who were in TBS, basically run and operate the program with him supervising. The popular kids were the ones who voted themselves into the desired positions such as being the anchors, directors, and the face of TBS. They left all the non-desired positions for the less popular kids, but as the school year went on this became less of an issue. During this year, I began to feel unhappy because I knew I was not being myself in an effort to fit in. I looked at myself and thought that all of these people are nothing like me, why do I want to act like a judgmental and stuck-up person. It was an awakening to seeing the flaws and the fake environment I saw all of us living in. The popular kids would laugh at each other's jokes even if they weren't even close to funny. It was only the principle behind acknowledging that they were trying to sound funny and their friends would pretend like it was. It was a pathetic attempt at friendship in these certain groups. I often questioned myself when I came across these scenarios, such as when a guy would try to be funny and all the girls would laugh and I would think it really wasn't that funny, so I'm not going to laugh and act like it was. Or when people would talk about something that they're interested in and all their friends would try to chime in on why they liked that stuff too. I always thought, I know I don't have an interest in that, therefore I'm not going to act like I do to seem relatable to them. Everything was one big act in my eyes. I could tell most of the things they laughed at, the others didn't find it funny, they just didn't want to be left out of a joke. When one person would see their friend treat a less popular kid with a lower amount of respect, they would think that they need to treat people like that too because if they act like that, they'll fit in. It was a huge facade that I realized I wasn't going along with anymore. I was going to flip my reasons for my unhappiness because I wasn't going to stand lying to myself like that.

This caused a noticeable difference in my life, no longer was I feeling held down by protecting this fake persona I maintained. It was almost a night and day difference in how I acted around people past this point. I could care less about being a part of that ecosystem anymore. If I didn't think something was funny, I wouldn't pretend it was. I wouldn't sit there and agree with something if I didn't truly agree with them. I wasn't going to treat a less popular kid with any lower amount of respect than I treated my best friends, because that's how life works if people are nice to you. I saw the lack of individuality within these kids and I was embarrassed for them because I knew that's not who they wanted to be. They just didn't have enough courage to be themselves. Without a doubt, I could tell that the popular kids saw that I wasn't going along with them, which inevitably put me out of their social circle. There were guys who acted like the definition of despicable because they thought they were better than everyone and the girls acted like they were too exclusive to talk to anyone outside of their friend group. I could call some of those people out on how careless they treated others and how poor their personalities are, but that's not what this book is for.

There was one guy named Trevor who was more or less in the popular group, but he was the nicest guy I ever came across in TBS. He was kind to you no matter who you were and that went a long way with me, given our environment. TBS was one of the best things I ever did in school. Not only did it expose me to the politics within social groups, but I never had so much fun enjoying all the projects and video work for the class. I don't even want to know what kind of budget our school had to fund this program, but we had full range of learning how to operate an intermediate level switchboard, teleprompters, professional studio cameras, handheld cameras, mics, a green screen, and multiple monitors for recording the broadcasts and burning them onto CDs. Not to mention we also went on numerous field trips to radio station studios, popular landmarks, and the state capital. It was a full-on news broadcasting team run by middle schoolers. We recorded live morning broadcasts that played on every smartboard in a classroom. We had made many intros that were based on popular TV shows such as *One Tree Hill, Full House,* and *The Office,* which showcased everyone who was a part of TBS. We also made funny videos and light-hearted skits that played after or during the morning broadcasts. A couple of the videos we did were called "JMS Scholars" and a comedy skit titled "2 Men, 1 Job." JMS Scholars was an interview-style video I got to host, where I went around interviewing kids at our school with a list of trivia questions. It was hilarious when I would ask "How many stars are on the American flag?" or "What countries border the United States?" and people would go blank and have no clue because they were put on the spot. Though there were a few people who almost got every question correct. 2 Men 1 Job was a comedy skit by Jackson and I where it was based in the broadcasting room. The plot was there was a broadcast to do, but it was only Jackson and I in charge of filming it. The song "Yakety Sax" played as we scrambled all over the broadcasting room struggling to film, anchor, report weather, and read the news in quick succession. That was one of the funniest videos we did and it took a while to film because we all couldn't stop laughing about how ridiculous it was.

There were also a ton of perks that came with being in this program. We were sometimes allowed to be excused from class after our work was complete so we could "work on a project for TBS." Which was true in most cases, but it later got abused by everyone and some of the teachers didn't like TBS because it gave kids an excuse to leave their class. I left my history class a bunch for TBS because the teacher was lax about us leaving once we completed our work for the day. I would go in there and hang out with people that didn't have class as well. Trevor was in my same history class and we often went to TBS and hung out while listening to music through the room speakers. Once we were in TBS for a while, we even started not eating in the lunchroom anymore because we were allowed to come into the engineering room to eat and that's exactly what we did. A bunch of people from TBS would come in during these lunch periods. Jon, Jackson, and I were the last group to eat. Every single day, I would get my lunch and make my way up to the engineering room. I would then meet up with Jon and Jackson and we would go into the computer room where we would watch shows on YouTube. The two major shows that kept us dying laughing the whole year were *Video Game High School* and *Enter the Dojo*. I would be sitting there in the cozy dark room eating my chicken nuggets, laughing my head off on the newest episode of *Enter the Dojo*. Every day they came out with a new episode and every Friday we watched *Video Game High School*.

There were countless funny moments during TBS that I could make a sitcom based on this class. One day we were getting ready for our scheduled broadcast and before the broadcast started we always went over everything to make sure we had our video segments in order, made sure the cameras work and checked the sound. I was helping make sure the cameras worked, while Jackson stayed behind the monitor and saw if it was on. Our switchboard allowed us to see what was being filmed without it being broadcasted in the classrooms unless the transition lever was switched on. Us all thinking the lever was switched off, I got up close to the camera and started wagging my tongue around like a dog. We were all laughing hysterically, while this one football player sat at the teleprompter desk and scowled at us like he was too cool for our shenanigans. Jackson looked over in shock and realized the lever was switched on. That whole time the whole school could see my dog-wagging tongue in full view. I was kind of embarrassed at first, but it was pretty hilarious so we figured the rest of the school got a laugh from it as well. Mr. Ravenscroft often gave us video ideas to film for TBS. One video we worked on, but sadly never got to air, was a short horror film. It was based on the mysteries and rumors of the third floor. The third floor was like the Bermuda Triangle or Area 51 of our school. No one was allowed to go up there and nobody knew what they kept up there. We had permission and the great privilege to be able to go there and film for this video. The only way up was through an elevator, which already was off-limits for students. It was a dark, cold, and spooky open floor. We were able to witness firsthand what many students dreamed about seeing. In short, it was essentially a storage room, but it still possessed a sense of creepiness, mystery, and odd dusty objects scattered on the floor. There were no lights, black walls, concrete floor, and an eerie aroma, perfect for filming a horror film. We had written out a whole script and filmed a few scenes, but later were told for some reason the video would never get the chance to air. I was just happy to be able to experience the third floor and its untold mysteries.

Our last and final project for TBS was our school's "Lip Dub." This was essentially our "end of the year celebration video." Many schools were doing this at the time and it was where a camera went around the whole school as students took turns singing the background music and showcasing many of the groups and clubs the school had. For a better example, look up "Lip Dub" on YouTube and that's what we had to do. The best part about it was that Jon, Jackson, and I were given the task to produce and direct it. The lip dub was our biggest project yet and was going to take many hours of planning, rehearsing, and revising. For weeks, we got together during our TBS hour and went around the school mapping out the route of the lip dub. We tried to perfectly synchronize the songs when a different part of the school would begin singing. It was a wild amount of preparation for this video that was destined to be one of the best produced lip dubs out of any school. Towards it getting closer to the film date of the video, we got word that the head of the school was going to scratch our plan and come up with their own version. We felt completely disregarded to the fullest. I remember us even pleading to Mr. Ravenscroft, that he could pass on the principles that our plan was so well constructed it would be almost impossible to beat. We had done so much hard work and were given a great responsibility for this whole operation, only to be brushed off like it was nothing by the end of it all. I have no idea how the school came up with a whole new plan for the lip dub just days before the video. The day came and our film crew got into position and the whole school flooded the hallways. There was a small briefing to the students on how the video was going to go and it had to be done in one take. The record button was pushed and on went the official recording day of our schools lip dub. One hallway after another, the camera guys went filming the singing students and staff members. After we had finished the video, I remember re-watching it in the TBS room and talking with Jon and Jackson on how our version would've been better, but our school didn't want to trust a few 15 year olds to direct a musical. Towards the end of TBS, we had a few kids from the previous grade begin to enroll and sign up. One of the new kids that signed up was Jack Haines, a bright kid with a likeable personality. This is where Jack first met Jon, Jackson and I and would later become a long term friend of ours.

The school year was almost over, but I've got a funny story regarding this upcoming summer. I had asked out this girl right before the school year ended. She and I had been great childhood friends since fourth grade. During middle school, we rode the same bus and would talk every day on the way to school. By the end of middle school, I figured we had become such good friends that I might as well see if she wanted to date me. This is why I wanted to mention it was not the best idea because depending on how the relationship went, it could either help or hurt the existing friendship. But I took the chance anyway because it seemed like she liked me and I liked her. We hung out a lot outside of school such as riding bikes and going out places with our friends. Sometime in one of the last weeks of school, we were out riding bikes and it started pouring rain. I had already planned on asking her out, I was just waiting for the right time. We took shelter under a canopy of trees in the neighborhood that briefly shielded us from the rain. I figured this was the right time to ask her out, given we were stuck there waiting for the rain to die down. I stood up and told her I wanted to ask her something,

"Will you go out with me?"

She kind of smiled and then it transitioned to an expression of hesitancy. She briefly told me it wasn't a good time, partially because of her busy schedule with Pom and it was best to wait a couple weeks. Me being the person to not give up on the things I want, of course I would try again in a couple weeks if that's what it was going to take! Or I could've taken that as a sign to back out from it and continue to be great friends with her, but I felt like this was bound to happen at some point so why not go for it. Once summer began, we had hung out a few times and one time I invited her to go see a movie with me. The newly remastered horror film "Poltergeist" had just come out and we both enjoyed horror movies so I thought it would be a perfect time to ask the question after the movie. The date went rough, there was no one in this theatre and we barely talked during the whole movie, making it awkwardly quiet until we got up and left. As we were walking out of the theatre and her mom was almost there to pick her up, I stopped and got her attention. I then asked her out for the second time and I gladly got a completely different response then the last. She was beyond happy and said yes with confidence. I was pretty satisfied to say the least; school was over and I got a girlfriend? Heck yeah!

So that's it? Middle school came and went and now only part of a book? Essentially yes, but it gave me such useful fundamentals going forward in my life that I'll further improve on in the upcoming years. This is also where I would come to meet some of my first actual friends that I'd come to spend the rest of high school with. It's crazy how your seating arrangement in school can literally change your life. Just like that, middle school was in the past and the summer of 15' would welcome me with open arms. I started summer off with a week-long trip to Colorado with my family. Going to Pikes Peak, visiting Estes Park, and even stopping by a skatepark were some of the activities we did there. The rest of summer was spent hanging out with Truman, Jackson, and Jon. Skylar had moved to Florida after school ended and we rarely hung out with Andrew outside of school, hence it was mainly the four of us hanging out. On days I didn't spend skating, we would hang out at Jon's house, and sometimes Truman and I would go to the skatepark. Jon got the idea of starting a podcast with the four of us, since we now had more free time. Based on the aspirations from TBS, we were going to have our own show with the four of us. We called it "JMS Podcast" where we sat at a table in Jon's basement and talked about the things we liked and new things coming out. "Fast & Furious 7" had just come out and we had recently seen it in theatres, that was one of our topics we covered in the first episode. One weird roadblock we ran into was there was another YouTube channel with the exact same name of the podcast. They emailed Jon telling him that we were going to sue if we didn't change the name. Through back and forth emails, we came to an agreement and we were able to keep the name with no legal risks on us. We continued this podcast on and off the rest of summer until we slowly stopped doing them. In the last few weeks of summer, I continued skating with Truman and playing Call of Duty for hours. The girlfriend and I were on a slow decline into the bottom of a fictional river. Once again I'll mention, it cracks me up thinking about 15 year old me dating this girl. Though I think it's good behavioral practice for the real deal later in life. I could tell she had lost interest in me and at the time it hurt a little bit, but I just knew I'd be set free from the imaginary obligations as a boyfriend. We met up on our bikes and agreed to go back to being friends. Yep, I definitely should've not asked her out the second time.

School was starting in a few days and I remembered a time when Truman's mom was driving us back from the skatepark and she told us "high school is going to be so fun, you'll meet a lot of people, do a lot of things, go a lot of places, these will be one of the best four years of your life." I thought no way, this will just be another period of school I have to go through and it will be over. Oh was I wrong and those words of hers would soon be fulfilled.

6

Fresh Meat

The first year of high school rolled around and some of our friends went on their own journeys and some moved away. Though I still had the original four that I met in middle school. Freshman year consisted of diving head first into the pool of high school and all the endeavors that I was about to face. It was commonly known that Freshmen are considered "Fresh meat" like we were being fed to the sharks in the ocean of high school. In a way, it really does feel like that. I was like this little shrimp trying to find the right place to go, while looking at the great white sharks and barracudas we shared the school with. Thankfully I knew at some point or another I would be there too. The first half of freshman year was pretty casual, I met a few new people and also had the same lunch hour with Jon and Truman. I had signed up for the filmmaking and film studies class with Jon and Jackson. I thought this would be a great class as a form of continuation in film and media. The high school didn't have daily broadcasts like the middle school did, but we figured this was the next best thing. During the year, we were assigned to film and produce four documentaries in an interview style. This class was awesome; It was similar to TBS, but a bit more professional. Our class was split into multiple teams of two and my partner for the year was Jackson. We put together some superb films by the end of the year. We did a piece on the national landmark "The USS Batfish," a retired WWII navy submarine with a world record of sinking 3 submarines in 76 hours. Some of our other films included a famous pumpkin patch, a talented sign spinner, and a heartwarming story about a little girl battling Retinoblastoma. The teacher, Mr. Raphael, is also a great guy. Being well known for teaching his award-winning film students to victory across the nation. A running joke we got from this class, that we still reference from high school, is a phrase that Mr. Raphael called one of Jon's films. Jon had made a piece that same year about Truman's inspirational story about his passion for skateboarding called "Limitless." This was one of Jon's better produced films in the class because of the structure of the interviews and the incredible cinematography he did. Our teacher was so impressed with the film he jokingly stated "This is something straight out of a Spielberg movie." We laughed so hard because we never would've guessed our film teacher would complement Jon like that, it was just funny the way he said it. From then on, we've always referenced that phrase in watching movies and other times in our life by saying "Man that was straight out of Spielberg!" Not many people know about that joke, so don't tell anyone! Another one of my favorite classes that I signed up for freshman year was "Technology Student Intern" or TSI for short. It was a hands-on technology class where I did repairs on hardware and software on school-owned computers that were provided for the students. I've always been interested in technology and this class was great for immersing me in that field. Oklahoma history was not something I particularly wanted to take, but it was required to graduate. The teacher who taught it was a young woman with a pointy nose and long red hair. She seemed nice at first, but soon revealed her defensive and know-it-all personality. I am the younger one in this case, but I know a bag of wind when I see it. Throughout the year I remained cooperative and got all the assignments done accordingly. Towards the end of the year there was a fairly large assignment that I was working towards. I had gotten sick and had to miss one single day of school. She had changed the due date on that day from what I had previously known. I kept working on the assignment thinking it was due later, she then told us it was due at the end of the week. I thought how come I didn't know about this? Then it clicked, in the time I was gone, I had missed her updated information about the assignment. I tried to finish what I could by then but it was too far gone, I had to turn it in partially completed. I sent her an email apologizing for completing the assignment inadequately, hoping she could find some sympathy. Unfortunately, that was not the case; I get an email back that is written in a unique tone of sarcasm. Something along the lines of "I can't do anything to help your poor time management, I even found some websites to help you with that," followed by several time management websites. I knew at the end of the day it wasn't a time management issue, but I digress.

The Hot Sauce Pack went to the color war once again with Jackson that year and little did I know it was the last time I'd go for a long time. Nothing beats the first time when Skylar and Andrew were still in the group and we all looked like first graders. The color war that year was great but it was good that I had a fun time that day because two days later, after the color war, I was getting my wisdom teeth taken out. Getting my wisdom teeth out was one of the weirdest challenges I've ever faced. I oddly never had any pain in my teeth leading up to the operation. Some people wait for their wisdom teeth to begin to come up, causing discomfort leading to eventual removal. Others are lucky enough to have a big enough chomper to not even need theirs out. During my usual dentist appointments, he pointed out that mine were coming in and supposedly it's not a bad idea to remove them before the roots form. Mine also happened to be a rare case where I had one extra wisdom tooth on my bottom left side, making it five total. I was slightly scared to have it done because I'd seen some videos of people I knew after getting theirs out and they look like zombies with drool, blood, and cotton coming out of their mouth. The comforting fact with getting my wisdom teeth out was that they'd put me to sleep like a sloth after a full course meal. It was September 18th 2015 on a Friday at 9:30am, the only reason I remember that so clear is because that's all I thought about for 3 weeks straight. The day came and I was quite calm going into it, usually I have a little dentist anxiety. I sat in the chair in a dim-lit room and they put the IV in my arm. The main doctor came in and put one of the comfiest blankets I've ever felt on me. He then sits down and talks to me, waiting for me to go to sleep.

"Do you have any pets?" he asks.

"No, but I'd like to have one, one day."

He then tells me what kind of dog he has and talks a bit more. Then it came time.

"Alright I'm going to have you count to ten out loud for me" he told me.

I'm not even kidding when I say this, but I was still wide awake when he told me this. I was there thinking just 10?, that's it?. In the moment I felt like I could count to 100 with no problem, that's how awake I felt. This will be the easiest counting to ten in my life.

"One, two, three, fou-" I woke up and it was over. I didn't even finish the word four and it was already done and I was being carted out in a wheelchair to my mom's car. I was singing Elvis Presley on the ride home, not really registering what was going on half the time. My jaw felt like Mike Tyson had used it as a punching bag. My diet consisted of applesauce and Snack-Pack chocolate pudding for the next three weeks. I went to a car show with Truman that following Sunday and in one of the pictures you can see my cheeks look like I'm storing food for the winter.

A few months later during school, I would come to meet Landon who was good friends with my friend Brandon from fifth grade, and Brandon introduced me to him. Landon had similar characteristics to a skater like long wavy hair, only wore vans, and was into longboarding. He was the one who introduced me to longboarding and that's where I found a new hobby with the extension from skateboarding. Longboarding is a more elegant style of skateboarding in a way, there are rarely any flips, smoother of a ride, and a bit easier to control because of its larger surface. I bought a used board from a friend and that's what got me started. I enjoy longboarding because it's different enough from skateboarding to separately enjoy it. You can wear gloves so you're able to put your hands down for slides and make the wheels perform more towards speed or smoothness. It's a fascinating sport that I was glad to pick up.

Around this same time, I had also met a new friend of Truman's, named Zach. Zach was a wild kid when I first met him, he was exclamatory and had a thundering presence with him. He also was slowly getting into cars and Truman and I would often be reminding him of car lingo so he could understand us when we were talking about them. Truman, Jon, Zach, Landon, Brandon, and I all had the same lunch hour and we had a specific table we sat at each day. We established this group of the six of us called

"The Fury Crew," though this group didn't go too far outside of the lunchroom. We began having roast battles to see who could diss each other the best, that was easily my best memory from freshman year. Roasting people became popular and we carried that trend to our lunch table every Friday. Every single week for a solid two months or so, we would have these roasts battles. I even made posts on Instagram like an advertisement about when and where we would have them. We usually went in a clockwise rotation around the table as we said a segment of roasts for about a minute. After each roast, we would rate how good or bad the roast was, depending on the reaction of the table. Our roasts mainly consisted of ones attacking personal attributes like hair, face, and personality. It was a brutal test to see how much jokingly verbal abuse one could take. Though we had stated before ever doing this that all of us didn't truly mean what we said, we were just trying to be as rough as possible to make it more entertaining. No one ever got seriously upset or offended by the end of it. I pre-wrote almost every roast I ever said because I had trouble coming up with ones on the spot and it made for better, more thought-out roasts. I even added names at the bottom for who I thought the roast would be more effective towards. I'll read a few off my phone that I still have saved from December 2015.

"You need braces because all your teeth are messed up, speaking of braces your breath smells like ketchup. Why you got all that hair? Are you trying to cover up that makeup? Now I know why all your girls gave up."

"My roast will make you sick, looks like you're already turning green. Your face looks funny like the duck from kids' cuisine. Your name should be Eugene because only nerds have the d*ck size of a jelly bean."

I'm sorry if your name is Eugene, but I had to come up with something that rhymed. Believe me, there were some that are much worse as far as vulgarity and hurtfulness goes. I'll leave that up to your imagination on what 15 year old boys can insult each other with.

Winter break came and before I knew it, we were back to school. In my computer fixing class, TSI, we got a second teacher to help out in the office. Her name was Dawn and one thing that stood out to me was that she was quite young to be a teacher. Most of my school teachers were well into their 40's and 50's. Since she was only twice my age, this is where I thought we could get along with ease. The end of January, came with a slight surprise to spice up my life. Ben and I were hanging out down by the creek outside of the waterfall cliff. It was in the evening time and we were out walking around. Occasionally I liked to jump over things, such as fire hydrants, generators, and really anything that was waist height. There was about a three foot tall vented electric post with a cap on it. I don't know what the exact name of it is, but they're found in many yards and fields above the ground. I went to casually leapfrog over it and somehow my right thumb got caught at the top of it. At the moment it didn't feel like I did anything to it. I may have thought it hurt a little bit, but I brushed it off and continued hanging out with ben. After a short time I could tell the pain wasn't going away and I began to wonder if I had done something besides just a scuff. I told Ben that my thumb was still hurting and I remember him telling me "Ah you're fine, it doesn't look bad." I wanted to believe him but I just had a feeling it was something more. I could feel a feeling of separation of the bone every time I pressed on my thumb. I went home and told my parents what happened and we came to a conclusion to go get it checked out. I could tell they also thought it wasn't broken or anything further than a bruise. We got my thumb X-rayed and the doctor came into the office after examining it. Believe it or not, I had actually broken the tip of my thumb. Who does that? Who do you know that they've broken the tip of their thumb before? My mom to no surprise was perplexed on how the heck I even did this. After countless times I've jumped over those things before, the snake finally bit me. Since it was a pretty small break I didn't have to have a cast, they just gave me a hand brace that secured my thumb. Luckily this was on my right hand this time, so my writing wasn't interfered with.

Jackson showed Jon and I this photography app, using animated GIFs, that was growing in popularity. It was called "Phhhoto." We pronounced it in all sorts of ways like "Pha-ho-toe," "Ph-h-h-oto," or just simply "Photo." We never learned how to actually pronounce it, but it didn't matter if we enjoyed it. This app gave us a new purpose of exploring and using the environment to capture natural art. Since they were GIFs that could add filters to, we got creative with how to take these pictures. We went all around neighborhoods and places around town seeing what we could make with our surroundings. The Arkansas River is a great big body of water that, where we saw it, would get incredibly shallow and sometimes almost look dry. There is about a mile long bridge that goes over the river and underneath it the river would dry up for miles in both directions. We decided that would be an awesome idea to go explore, as well as capturing pictures for Phhhoto. We walked down the rocky banks down to the river. We walked around for hours, running and jumping, enjoying the freedom of being able to walk on a river that was so vast. I thought it was amusing to think that the next time it rained that water would probably be above our heads. We took some pictures and walked around some more before heading home. People at our school began to catch wind of this app and there was a group of older kids that wanted to host a Phhhoto meetup. They already had a decent following on the app so this was more or less an event to promote collaboration and encourage people to join them. Jon, Jackson, and I were super interested because we thought no one at our school knew about this app. It also brought out people from around the state to come meet each other. We met downtown and from there we were told to go to the Philbrook museum where we would continue to take pictures and draw inspiration from. I didn't talk much to the people who hosted it, it was more an opportunity to hang with Jackson and Jon at this meet. We walked around and explored the expansive art museum as the day started to wrap up. Who knew walking around all day looking at art and taking pictures would make me tired.

Summer was on the horizon and I always get excited because that means less school and more spending time with my friends. Both Jon and Jackson happened to introduce me to the perfect drinks to enjoy during the summer and eventually year-round. A few months prior Jon had told us about the soda drink "Jones" that he discovered from a former place where he lived. The drink hooked me instantly and the next time we came across one in the store I made sure to try it. The drink is amazing, the labels are creative, and they have little messages under the cap. Jackson had shown us "Arizona Tea." I had seen them before but never paid much attention. Jackson had told us this is one of his favorite drinks and said this is a must-have for summer endeavors. It was the same feedback I had as Jones, the flavors and labels are ingenious and the price is the best part, 0.99 cents for a tall can. My favorite flavors I mainly stick to are Grapeade and Watermelon, it really is heaven in a can. Most of the times we hung out, we would go to the corner store on our bikes and skateboards and grab Jones and Arizona's with some snacks. One of our popular spots to hang out at was this school playground that was down the street from Jon and I. Jackson, Jon, and I were hanging at this school and occasionally we would get on top of the roof part of the school that was about a story or two off the ground and continued higher in some places. One time we were hanging out in the parking lot and I went up and climbed up to the very top of this roof. As I'm sitting on the top, watching Jon and Jackson hang out in the parking lot down below, I see a campus police car drive into the parking lot. Immediately I panicked because I thought that he had seen me climb up there because of how short it was that he showed up. I proceeded to run to the back of the roof and try to make it down that way. The only way to get up on the roof and down was the same side that the cop, Jackson, and Jon were talking on... so I thought. I had the idea to go off of the backside of the building, I made my way down to a point where it was about 15-feet off the ground and I jumped off of the roof. I took a chance if it was going to hurt my ankles or not, but once I landed, I realized I was fine. To waste time, I ran around the entirety of the school looping back to the parking lot where Jon and Jackson were. Jackson told me that the cop just wanted to stop by and see what we were doing and he had no idea and I went up on the roof. With a big sigh of relief that I wasn't going to jail that day, I was happy and my ankles remained intact

I was longboarding quite often, about as much as I did skating. Zach was also starting to get into longboarding because he had skated a little bit growing up. He told me there was this big longboard race from one side of town to the other. I was so stoked, I've never been in any type of longboard race, but I knew they existed. Neither of us could drive so we had Zach's brother run us down where it was in his 1990's Volvo 850 sedan. The air conditioning didn't work and it was an extremely hot day in May. Riding down the road, I remember thinking I could not wait to get out of that car, even with the windows down. We showed up and the race was well past the start, we figured we might as well try to catch up. We saw where the group of participants were, but there was a whole river in between us. The race started on one side, crossed a half-mile bridge, then went back down the other side where the finish line was. As soon as we got dropped off, we got our boards out from the trunk and began running to the path to start on. Pushing as fast as we could down this path, I knew that it was almost impossible to get any respectable position in this race, but at least we could say we were there. The pavement on the path was smooth, which made it a lot easier to acquire and maintain speed. After we crossed the bridge that wasn't so smooth, my legs began to wear out. It being extremely hot, was taking a toll on my stamina and that's the point I was getting to. After 20-30 minutes of hard pushing, we took short breaks and gave up on the fact that we would come nowhere close to the huge group. We decided to take a shortcut back to where we came from and call it a day. Once we made it back to where we started, we began filming clips of us trying to powerslide. I got a few mediocre slides down then Zach went. Behind the camera I tracked Zach as he came down the path where we did our slides. The run-up was looking good, but he got a little wobbly, back foot slipped off, the board shot out, lost his balance and smacked the back of his noggin. It was at a pretty low speed, but I still felt bad because it looked like it hurt. Thankfully he seemed alright after taking a break for a few minutes. Being a skater you will take a lot of falls and especially in longboarding where it's usually at high speeds. I encourage everyone to wear a helmet. You can get away with it in skateboarding because most of the time it's lower speeds and low impact, unless you're jumping down huge stairs sets or handrails. In longboarding there is little you can do to prevent being thrown off. We skated around a bit more until heading home to cool off and let our legs recover. Sometime after this race I was introduced to the one and only, pasta-loving, glasses-wearing, car-loving, Rogers. Rogers was great friends with Truman and Zach through school. I didn't hang out with Rogers much at the beginning, but this is when we met for future context.

Getting behind the wheel of a car was a magical experience in the near future of high school. Truman was the first person in the group to get a car and get his license. Us being car guys, we couldn't wait for the day to start modifying our cars. Truman's first car was a 2006 Pontiac Grand Prix sedan, the perfect sized car to fit us all in for our adventures. We plasti dipped the wheels, installed red interior lights, and we even cut the exhaust off with a metal saw that was not meant for exhaust cutting. At times we tried brainstorming any possible mods to do to the Pontiac. At one point when we were hanging at Truman's house, he said "I have some spare wireless Christmas lights we could try to put on." So that's exactly what we did. We got some tape, got the lights, and taped that sucker underneath the front bumper. Even at 15 we thought it was pretty silly looking, but it was worth a try to see what it looked like. We valued this car as the first official car in THSP. Zach also got his first car around the same time, a silver 90's Volkswagen Golf Mk3, and named it Laphonda. This became a one of a kind car in our group with outstanding 90's characteristics. Zach loved that car like it was a family member, as later did we all. Sometimes when we hung out at Zach's house, we would occasionally take Laphonda out around the block and down a few roads, even when he didn't have a license. What also made driving exciting for us is that we were all obsessed with drifting and extreme motorsports. One key aspect about drifting is that it's a lot easier to have a rear-wheel-drive car, but as you'll see later, we made do with front-wheel-drive cars. Truman, Zach, and I piled in the Golf one day and headed down the road. The rattling of metal and old plastic interior pieces always reminded us it was a 90's car. Zach also raced dirt bikes and four-wheelers growing up, therefore he had a bit more experience behind the wheel than Truman and I did. There were a few corners near his house that had a little bit of dirt and gravel on them. Without warning Zach yanked up the E-brake handle and out went the back end of the car at 20 mph. It was an immediate shift in weight as Truman and I got sucked to the left side of the car. It was amazing, this was one of the first times in my life where we got a taste of drifting a car. Up the road there was an industrial building with a gravel parking lot. Pulling the E-brake on a car is a lot less harmful on the mechanism when it's on a loose surface such as gravel, dirt, or heavy rain. We pulled into the gravel lot and Zach got a small amount of momentum and up went the E-brake. We went sliding like a 2000 pound hockey puck, we slid as the gravel was shot up behind us. After fooling around a bit more, he did a small burnout and off we went. The Golf had made a great first impression, but that was only a taste. Sometime later Zach got the idea of making the Golf louder, most of our cars were loud and he wanted to make his loud as well. When we were 16 we came with many "on-the-spot ideas" when it came to modifying cars. Jon, Truman, and I were hanging out at Zach's house when Zach got the idea to drill holes into the exhaust pipe to make it loud without the need of buying anything. We had tried unbolting the exhaust, but the pipes were so rusty they were practically welded on. Zach went back into his garage and searched around for some tools that could help. He came out with a cordless drill with a step-down bit. He pressed hard on the drill and tried as hard as he could to break through the hardened rusted pipe. It was difficult to drill a large hole with the bit, so he drilled lots of small holes all along the pipe. I looked down there after hearing him basically saw the car in half and it looked like the exhaust pipe was Swiss cheese. We all were laughing hysterically once he fired it up and had successfully made his car louder from taking a makeshift hole puncher to the exhaust several times. In honor of Zach achieving this profound innovation, we ended the night off by getting in the back of his dad's work truck and collectively sang the song "Sweet Caroline" by Neil Diamond.

We got word that there was a weekly car show going on in a parking lot outside a local restaurant. They were every Tuesday around 6pm and usually had about 40-70 cars ranging from classic muscle cars, JDM, and the occasional Lamborghini. The best part about this meet was that we could get free sweet iced tea. Not many people knew about this, but you could go into the restaurant and say you were there for the car show and they would give you a free sweet iced tea. Also right across from the car meet was a Sonic drive-in, sometimes I would grab a burger from Sonic, get my free sweet tea, and enjoy the scenery of some of Oklahoma's coolest cars.

Jackson, Jon, Truman, and I enjoyed watching movies. It was an easy idea for hanging out and not too expensive. During the school year and into summer we watched several of the new ones that came into theatres. One movie that we had built up a lot of anticipation for was the skateboarding film "We Are Blood." It didn't come out in theatres, but was alternatively released for online purchase. It had been a while since the last well-produced cinematic skateboarding film was made, but this looked to be up next. We were so excited to finally see this masterpiece of a movie. We watched it the first time at Jon's house and I bought it on iTunes to then watch it multiple times over. It was one of the best skateboarding films I've ever watched, the music, shots, skaters, it was all amazing. The production value of this skate film was unmatched from all the skate films I had watched. Along with watching movies, we also goofed around in the theatre from time to time. Jon, Jackson, and I went to see a movie and it was nobody but us in the whole theatre. So what do three freshman guys do when there's nobody in the theatre? I ran up and down the stairs as fast as I could, then I went across the rows of chairs screaming and jumping and occasionally laughing when Jon saw me acting like a monkey with too much caffeine. I hoped there was no one above in the camera room because they definitely would've thought I put something in my popcorn.

It was May and not only did that mean the beginning of summer, but it's also my Birthday month.

My family and I often went to go watch dirt track racing on the weekends. I thought for my sixteenth birthday I could invite Jon, Truman, and Jackson to watch the races with us. During the races we noticed there was a car in the back that was lagging behind, number 22. We thought it would be funny if we rooted for 22 to win, of course it was more than unlikely, but the underdog still had a chance. The laps kept going and 22 was not making up any ground. I'm not sure if his car just wasn't running right or just was an inexperienced racer. It was hilarious, all of us were in the stands screaming and hollering

"Let's go 22 woo!!"

"You got this dude!"

People were probably thinking why the heck are these guys rooting for the car all the way in the back. After the race, of course we had to get a group picture with the legend itself, the number 22 car. We went into the pits and found the car, Jon and I on the left, Truman and Jackson on the right. We still joke about the great effort that car had, no matter how far behind he was, the car still finished the race.

What also comes with turning sixteen is the privilege of getting a car. I was blessed to be the second owner of my grandma's 2004 Toyota Avalon. I was super excited about getting ready to have my own car to be able to modify. At the time, I rarely thought about the authenticity of things. All day at school I would be researching and discovering what possible aftermarket parts I can put on the car. I'm glad my parents didn't allow me to carry out all my plans because I would've ruined that car. Just some of the things I had planned on doing included: Hood pins, air to fuel ratio gage, oil pressure gauge, tachometer, all of which are completely unnecessary for that car. Though I did get away with a few things that would keep the car's originality in the end. My parents made a deal with me, I can do anything as long as it can go back to stock form. Basically everything in between permanent painting or cutting. The creativity went flowing onto a sheet of paper. The more realistic modifications I planned on doing were small cosmetics like a front tow strap, bolt on muffler, JDM style fog lights, seat covers, and a lot of Plasti Dip. All of which I would later add during the summer. There's a unique philosophy behind modifying a car as a kid and maybe you can understand why me and my friends did this. Imagine you're in a position where you can't get the dream car you want. Being at a young age with not a lot of money, it could be years and years away until you're at that point in your life where you're able to have those cool cars. The inspiration and motivation is so strong, that you face the fact of trying to make the car you have into the car that you want. That is why all these cheap universal products for cars exist, so they can temporarily fill those wants until you eventually have that car you've always wanted. I tried coming up with all sorts of things to do to my car regardless if it was practical or not and that's the fun of modifying cars. Even being on a smaller scale, I would still have to find a way to fund my hobby and this was only the beginning.

One day towards the end of June, Truman, Zach, and I were hanging out at Rogers' house and it had just rained the night before. We all were in Rogers' room when someone suggested the idea of wanting to try drifting on the large puddles on some back roads by Rogers' house. We all were onboard with it and we piled into Truman's Pontiac. We were driving around trying to find the best place that had enough water on a corner. We came across an S-shaped road that had patches of water puddles all throughout it, perfect setup for drifting. We drove through it a few times to get the feel of how to initiate the drifts, then he went for it. The car had a pedal E-brake, which is a bit more difficult to engage and disengage than a regular handbrake. He was able to successfully drift a few of the turns and we were all screaming with excitement in the car. The next few tries were a bit patchy. The water was getting low and the tires got warmer, meaning there was more traction. He got some speed into a small corner, pulled the E-brake, rear end slid out, but immediately caught back traction. This snapped the steering the opposite way of the turn, sending the car into the curb and up over the grass going into a small ditch where it was stopped by a fence. It was wild how it happened so quickly and right as the car hit the curb, Rogers and I bounced up off the seats. Once I realized the car was no longer on the road and up against a fence, we had to get creative if we wanted no one to know about this. Truman was fairly upset, as I would be too if I was in his place. The bad part was that there were four of us and he could only legally drive one other person, so if Truman's dad had to come help, two of us had to get out of there. We first tried pushing it out of the ditch, Truman put it in reverse and the rest of us got up front giving it all we had. That didn't work so we had to call up Truman's dad. With him on the way, Rogers and I were the ones who had to leave, thankfully Rogers' house was close by so we walked through a neighborhood all the way back. During the walk, Rogers and I were talking back and forth like

"Wow, I can't believe that actually happened, that was crazy."

We didn't know what would happen next besides waiting for Truman to call us after they got the car out. Sure enough about 30 minutes later, we got a call from Truman saying they got the car free and were headed back to Rogers' house. It was safe to say that we didn't do any more drifting that day.

Later in the summer Truman had told me that he had this lake house that he spent a lot of time at during the summer and wanted to know if I were interested in going down there one weekend. I love anything and everything to do with the lake and I was more than happy to get the opportunity to join. It was awesome, a nice small house at the hop of a hill by a dirt road. He had all sorts of lake toys like a jet ski, four-wheelers, and a golf cart, all of which had some age on them. Truman seemed to be the king of his lake, he knew where every road went and how to get to places the fastest. I never had much experience on a four-wheeler or golf cart, but it was no problem after the first couple trails. I was familiar with my lake that my family visited often, but experiencing another lake of someone's familiarity is very satisfying. Truman went flying through the woods, obviously he was a more skilled four-wheel rider and I was impressed. I kept up fairly well after carefully maneuvering through the trees and over humps in the trails. The trails eventually lead out to a beach on one side of the lake. A mile-long huge stretch of sand was in front of me and it was like I had teleported to the coast of Miami. This is where we could go more open on the throttle. Off went Truman, speeding down the beach as I couldn't help but smile and then gun it right after him. In that moment I was thinking about nothing but the resistance in my hair from the lake air passing through. Truman explained to me that this beach is where a lot of people have bonfires and occasionally dock their boats. Truman also told me all the fun he and his cousins had playing games on the beach and racing four-wheelers. I once again felt thankful that I was able to experience just a small part of what Truman did growing up. We eventually went back to the house where we sat on the back porch drinking Sprite and eating grapes, trying to avoid getting stung by wasps. I often thought, man I could live like this forever but that was probably in-the-moment thinking, or was it?

7

The Ball Begins to Roll

The summer heat of 2016 was on the comedown. Sophomore year was here and I still had no idea what to expect. I was somewhat getting the hang of navigating through the school and began regularly hanging out with the members of The Hot Sauce Pack. I was still friends with everyone from The Fury Crew, but I rarely saw them anymore. This is when the great times and memorable adventures gained momentum, opposed to being limited from going places during freshman year. School became more of an ease, having already been at this campus for a year, all I had to worry about was completing more required classes. Aside from the basic classes, I had accounting, physical science, and TSI. Another great turn of events was my homeroom class got switched for some reason and I was with Truman and my great friend Brody who I had recently met. Soon after, I got to meet a couple of Brody's friends, Brayden and Spencer. Spencer was a fairly quiet kid with a friendly personality, while Brayden was a jokester kind of a guy with an awesome car. It was exactly what Truman had, but black with chrome wheels and the higher trim package V8 engine. Both these guys had no problem securing a place within our group. After school we would meet up with all of our friends in the parking lot and talk about school and cars. Most of our group had a great interest in cars and actively watched movies and TV shows relating to them, our favorite being Fast and the Furious. This is what partially made us all become great friends, that aspect of commonality within cars. I still have an iconic picture of us after school, replacing the muffler on Brody's car in his driveway.

After school one day, one of us had mentioned that there was a rare car in a neighborhood, so we planned to go check it out. On the highway heading towards the neighborhood, I was riding with Truman while Brody was riding with Brayden. Roll racing is a popular automotive activity by many, and being 16, we sometimes dipped our toes in the water. We lined up side-by-side going a set starting speed, then one person would honk three times and the race would begin. It stopped once a person would pull ahead a decent amount in front of the other car, declaring a victor. We did this a few times on the way there, Brayden having the faster car, won every time. We finally made it to the neighborhood where we came across the car in a dead end. It was a white 1990 Nissan 240sx hatchback, which happens to be my favorite car. After soaking in its glorified presence for a few minutes, we took a couple pictures with it and headed home. Except the racing wasn't over yet. On our way out of the neighborhood, there was a long stretch of road that was also wider than a regular neighborhood street. This time we raced in a "dig style," it would start from a complete stop, one person would sound off the three honks, and hammer the gas. The tires screamed while smoke started to form on the take-off, as I had the biggest smile and we were laughing the entire time. Thankfully this neighborhood did not have much activity going on so no one was at risk in this situation, but it still wasn't the smartest choice. We did a few more dig races for about 50 yards until finally leaving the neighborhood.

The sweet tea car meets were back in full swing and I tried to go every single Tuesday like it was a fixed schedule for me. At one of the meets some of us met a guy named Chris, he had an orange newer Honda Civic. Chris was in his late 20's but still managed to have relevant conversations with us, even though we were one year into high school. He was into end-of-the-world survival and always had a tactical machete in his trunk next to his car cleaning supplies. We also met a guy named John who was from the sunny state of California. John was like a cliche character in a surfing movie. He always wore Hawaiian shirts, flip flops, and a hula girl stuck to his dashboard. He looked like Tom Petty with shorter hair. Take a guess on what this guy drove, it was a light blue 1994 Honda Civic hatchback. He told us that it was his baby that he drove across the country from California to Oklahoma. John was a super cool guy to talk with when we did, he was always happy and having a good time. Sweet tea in one hand, shades on, and a cigarette in the mouth. These two guys became our new friends when we went to the Tuesday car meets. Even after the car meet was over and most of the cars had left, we would sometimes stick around a while longer. There were stray shopping carts in the parking lot from one of the stores and one time we got two of them, went to opposite sides, and ran them towards each other, sending the carts into one another to see how loud it would be. There also were other people who stayed after the show and would do huge burnouts because there were a lot less people. We always had a great time at these meets and continued to make memories every week.

Since Truman had his license for a while and I almost had mine, we tried thinking of new places to hangout outside of our neighborhood. One place that seemed kind of interesting to us, was a parking garage a few blocks away from our high school. It was tall and on the highest level, it had a great view of the city. We would drive up to the top, where we could gaze at the openness of the sky and the city while five stories above. We would come to spend a lot of time up here, talking and hanging out. All throughout high school, this became a popular spot for not only our friend group but many others later on. It then came time to get my license. I had confidence in my driving and I had passed the written test to get my permit on the first try. I felt like completing my drivers-ed class was more of an accomplishment than getting my license.

There was a girl driving, our instructor next to her, and this other guy and me in the back. He instructed this girl to merge onto the highway. As she was merging, there was a semi-truck in the lane to the left of us and there was a concrete wall to the right of us. Instead of yielding, she tried to beat the semi-truck. We were all yelling for her to stop as we thought we were going to get sandwiched by this truck into the wall. Thank goodness she was able to slow down fast enough and we snuck behind the truck with a few feet to spare. After that moment, I thought I was a better driver than Dale Earnhardt compared to her. When it came time to get my license, my mom and I showed up to the DMV at the crack of dawn and waited patiently for my time to take the test. An older fellow was in charge of being my instructor and there was not a chance he didn't internally judge the appearance of my car. He said "Alright we're going to pull out here and follow my instructions exactly where to go." We went down the road and through a neighborhood, occasionally telling me to stop and park alongside a curb. Then came the part of the test that everyone seemed more afraid of than anything, parallel parking. I drove into a parking lot that had a set of four cones on one side. I honestly was not sweating it in the slightest, I had practiced this a whole bunch before and I knew the dimensions of my car like the back of my hand. Whew, here we go Nick, pull the car past the cones, put it in reverse, cut the wheel hard, and ease it in there. After pulling a bit forward and straightening out the car, I had done it, flawlessly executed. When we got back, I looked out of the corner of my eye as he wrote some things down on the clipboard. He told me I had passed with a 100% success rate, I was beyond ecstatic. I had officially passed my driver's test and was ready to take on the road. One thing I was also thrilled about was being able to park in the spots at school where the older grade of car guys parked. I remember riding on the bus and seeing their cool modified cars backed in and parked along the backside of the parking lot. I thought as soon as I got my license that's where I'm going to park and that's exactly what I did.

It was known at our school that there was a place by a baseball field, hidden through a forest, that there was a big concrete structure on the edge of one side of the river; it was known as "The Wall." I had sort of known about this place, but we had recently heard about kids going back there to swim and party. Jackson and I were curious one day after school to go and check it out. Weaving through trees and weeds, we followed the path down to it. It finally led to the wall and there was even a ladder put down so we could get on top of it. It looked to be the remaining foundation to a railroad that previously went across the river. I climbed the ladder up to the giant structure, we took some pictures and added it to the imaginary "places to explore index." Another similar place we came across was called "The Slab." It was essentially a river runoff place with a slanted floor of concrete on one side. This is probably where the term came from, as it was quite literally a giant slab of concrete. We had heard that this was a popular smoking spot for kids at our school, but we wanted to check it out for ourselves and not for the purpose it was known for. To get to the spot, there was a trail through a forest with paint and art all on the trees. We followed the different colored stones until we reached the slab. The giant piece of concrete had been used as an art canvas by many, hundreds of spray-painted designs had covered the entirety of the concrete. I could tell why this was a popular place for kids to go because it was like a public art museum and it provided a great view of the river. After I found out about this place, I told the rest of our friend group that we should add The Slab to places that we hang out. We had days at school when class started much later so we had extra free time in the morning, this was called "Collaboration Day." On most collaboration days we would get donuts at the local donut shop and either hangout at the parking garage or go to The Slab. Nothing was better than getting 50 cent donuts and hanging with my buds before school started.

Around this time, Spencer unfortunately had to move to Kansas, but he had become such good friends with us that it wasn't the last time we would see him. Meanwhile in school, accounting was kicking my butt. I thought it was going to be fairly simple because all it seemed to be is adding and subtracting. Once I found out that I had to add and subtract from different accounts such as accounts receivable, payable, liabilities, and equity, it all started to get confusing. Especially after finding out Debit and Credit mean the opposite in accounting; that made it difficult to understand. The teacher was an awesome guy and had a super nice demeanor, but I had concluded that accounting wasn't going to turn out good for me if I stayed in the class the rest of the year. I made the executive decision that as soon as the semester was over, I would be gone with the wind. It's ironic because a lot of seniors were in that class taking it as a "blow-off class" to fill up their schedules. One of the guys that was in that class was a star baseball player for our high school and he was taller than a fully grown stick of Bamboo. I sat in the back of the class and every single day he would come in, take off his backpack, take off his hat, fluff his mullet, and take about 5 minutes to sit down. It was a daily routine that grew on me not to like this guy. He also gave our teacher a hard time on how boring the class was in a joking way, but our teacher let it slide because he was this valued athlete. Though this guy redeemed himself to me one day after class, when I saw him go out to his freshly painted old restored truck. It was a metallic orange and black two-tone paint design with nice chrome wheels. It was then when his truck made up for his cocky personality. My science class, on the other hand, was one heck of an experience. I had met a few good people along with some fairly wild ones. There was one kid who was in my science class and my math class who was beyond reckless. He went out of his way to show out if anyone dared him to do something. There were multiple times where when the teacher was out of the room, he would quickly hop up on the desk, and jump from desk to desk like they were lily pads, until purposefully body slamming into the last desk. Sometimes the huge desks would fall over from the impact and he would have to quickly pick them back up before our teacher came back. It was one of the funniest things I've ever seen at school. No one I've ever known would voluntarily jump on desks with all their body weight. Another kid in that same science class was a big partier and everyone knew that he did some crazy things on the weekends. One day we were doing a lab assignment that involved eggs. Somehow it was brought up that he was going to go to the bathroom and eat one of the raw eggs. A few people and I followed him in the bathroom and into one of the big stalls. He cracked open the egg and downed it like it was shot of alcohol as all us audibly cringed in disgust. After watching this kid casually down Chicken Little, it was as if nothing happened as we casually walked back to the classroom. At lunch a kid started to sit with us who I didn't particularly know too well, but he became a regular person at our lunch table, this was Charlie. Charlie was initially friends with Truman and Zach and got to meet most of us when he started eating lunch with us. I've told Charlie this before, but when I first met him I thought he was kind of weird and nerdy. Little did I know he would later turn out to be one of my best friends.

It was winter break for school and there were two things that made this one memorable. I had spent the majority of my time inside, but one of the days it had snowed a decent amount. A few of us decided that we wanted to go drifting in an open parking lot that was covered in snow and ice. I met up with Brody, Truman, Zach, and Jon around noon. Truman had a rope and sled in his car so we decided it would be a funny idea to pull someone on the sled as it's tied to Truman's car while going around this parking lot. We got it all tied up and ready for takeoff. I was one of the first to ride on the sled as Truman went around the parking lot at fairly low speeds. It felt so much faster than it really was, on the sled it felt like I was going about 40mph. With snow being shot up my sleeves and covering my face, it was time to pass on the torch. Zach was up to go next and I figured it would be a smart idea to ride in the trunk and watch Zach being pulled around by Truman. I hopped in the trunk as Zach sat down on the sled and it was off to the races. Truman did a few tight turns and went down the straight part of the parking lot. He then turned the car around and went back the way he came. As this was happening, he was struggling to gain traction on the snow so he instinctively gave it more gas. I was in the trunk laughing and having the greatest time, watching Zach hold onto the rope-like his life depended on it. Then all of a sudden there was a crash and the trunk lid above me came slamming down. I opened it back up and immediately was concerned. I got out and realized we had accidentally ran into one of the light poles that was in the parking lot. We weren't going any more than 10mph when we hit the pole, but it felt much faster. The mood of us all changed instantly from laughing to urgency. We all got out and looked at the damage, luckily it didn't look like anything was dented or anything happened to the pole. Truman lifted the hood and there was a little bit of smoke; once we saw that, we got a bit more worried. Then Truman noticed something that gave us all instant relief. The radiator cap popped off on impact and a small amount of the coolant had splashed onto the exhaust header, which made it smoke like water on a grill. Once we all knew the car was okay and we were too, we could then reflect on how hilarious it was. Brody was outside of the car filming us and he happened to capture the moment when we hit the pole. Watching it over and over, we couldn't stop laughing at how slow of an impact it was. A 3000 pound car gracefully sliding on the snow into a light pole, with Zach on the sled still moving.

My other memorable moment was on one of the days me, Truman, Jon, and one or two of our other friends got added to a group chat on Snapchat with a few girls we knew and some of their friends. Most of us didn't know why we were added to this group chat, everyone just went along with it as a chance to meet new people. Truman, Jon, and I only knew a couple of the girls. Everyone went back and forth talking for a few hours, sending memes, and talking about school. One of the girls stuck out to me, her name was Zoe. She was one of the girl's friends that I had met that night and I noticed her jokes were funnier than everyone else's. It's hard to describe how unique her tone was but I could tell Zoe was one of my favorite people in the group chat. After all of the people went to bed it was just Zoe and I talking back and forth.

She suggested the idea that we talk outside of the group chat because there was no point in texting six other people when it was just us. We stayed up for hours talking about a whole bunch of things related to getting to know each other like who our celebrity crushes were and what were our biggest fears. I don't think I would've had this strong of compatibility with any other girl in the group chat. It was getting late at night and we decided to go to bed. We kept texting almost everyday after that, getting to further know each other and talking about the things we were interested in. We had a similar taste in music and I kept thinking to myself, man this girl is incredible! I've never met anyone like this who takes the time to talk to me. It was pretty soon when we both admitted that we liked each other. It was one of those scenarios where I could totally see myself dating this girl, not to mention the fact I thought she was absolutely adorable. All factors were looking promising, until I discovered there was a detrimental interference with this storyline. I found out that she lived almost an hour away which would make it almost impossible to date because we'd rarely see each other. She told me it was almost a guarantee that we would date if we lived closer, which subconsciously destroyed me, knowing it was in reach but not quite there. We remained great friends and still frequently talked after that, but it took me a while to get over that it wouldn't work out. During this whole time I couldn't help but tell Jon and Truman about this because they were in the group chat when we all met. I remember having a bunch of talks with Jon about figuring out any possibility how it could work out and coming up with any realistic ideas. Jon and I were talking about it one day and he told me it would all be okay because if it was meant to work out, it would. I couldn't agree more with him and I had to go on knowing not to stress about it because I knew it was something that I couldn't change.

The need for exploration came once again. Truman, Jon, and I were having a blast finding new spots to hang out at. One place we had gotten the idea to explore was downtown. It wasn't too far from us and there were plenty of shops and things to do. We had seen some of the seniors were finding places around downtown that led up to rooftops of some of the buildings. Jon and I remembered from the Phhhoto meetup that there was a parking garage with a small building on top of it that had a ladder leading to the roof. We figured we would go and check it out to see how hard it would be to get on top. After driving up the six levels of this parking garage, there it was, the 15ft tall building extension with the ladder right on the front of it. It was chained up oddly, like they knew kids were doing this and tried to barricade it. There were no "No climbing" signs so we figured if anyone were to say something to us we could use that as an excuse. The ladder had immense structural integrity which gave me more confidence to climb it. One-by-one we went up the ladder, once we all got up there, it was like we had made it to the top of a mountain. Even though there were much taller skyscrapers around us, it still felt extremely fulfilling to be higher up than the top of this parking garage. I breathed in the downtown air as I looked around at all the buildings and structures below us. The sun was setting and I told Truman and Jon that this would not be the last time we would visit this spot.

The thrill of climbing things and discovering new places only went up from there. Truman, Jon, and I often drove by neighborhoods that were under construction and noticed that many of them were in the first stages of being built, leading us to think that nobody owned them yet. There were a few neighborhoods in the city that possessed many under construction houses. There was one neighborhood, away from the main road, that backed up to a church. This neighborhood had about five or six houses on the roughly five-acre plot of land. Once it got around nighttime we would go to each of these houses and see which one was the best to hangout in. Sometimes I went out by myself and looked for these houses for my personal record. I had a set criteria that I looked for in these houses, some had too much equipment in the house, too many nails and boards leading to the entrance, I wanted windows on all four sides of the house so I could clearly know what was surrounding the house. I preferred two story houses because of the height, but one story was okay. The jackpot houses were ones with a huge living room and the upstairs having a spacious room with a window having easy access to the roof. One house we found had exactly that; we parked down the street so it wasn't obvious that we were there and made our way in the house. Using the flashlight on our phones, we checked out the gigantic living room with marble countertops and made our way upstairs. We went up the wood plank stairs while we passed boxes of nails, saw dust, and gas station cups. We then made it into one of the rooms where it was as barebones as a room can get, white walls, white floor, and dust everywhere. The room had two large side-by-side windows that led out to the roof. We opened the window and climbed out onto the flat roof on the outside. It was effortless to make our way up to the top of the roof. Once the last person made it to the top, we just sat up there enjoying the view of the lit up church parking lot in front of us. It was like we were three birds sitting on a powerline, but on the top of this house. We sat up there for hours playing music, talking about school and what all was going on in our lives. We visited this house a bunch more times as a place to relax and hangout, knowing it was only a matter of time until the house was finished and we couldn't return.

Once most of our friend group had our licenses for a while, we began going to a popular car scene in town known as "The Need for Speed game in real life." It went down a busy strip of road called "Memorial," where people would race up and down this public road while people watched. This also gave it the name "Memorial Races." The most popular place to meet for these races was at a Sonic drive-in. At the drive-in, all of the coolest cars in Tulsa would meet and take up every parking spot at the Sonic.

They took place on Friday and Saturday nights from anywhere from 8 pm to midnight. Everytime we went there we would meet up with some of our friends and look at all the cars that came through. This place was where the more properly built cars were, ranging from 400-1000 horsepower cars that shook the ground when they went by. Sometimes the police would show up and try to kick everyone out of this Sonic, but there were hundreds of people and it never worked. The police also pulled tons of people over at this car meet, mostly for racing or burnouts. Some of my friends got tickets, but I always made sure to be extra careful when driving in that area. After seeing a glimpse of what went on at this car meet, this became a regular attraction for us to attend on the weekends.

Sometime in January, a few of us heard about the older kids at our school having bonfires down by the river. None of us knew where they were or when they had them, we just knew that it was going on. One kid we were distant friends with, who partied a whole bunch, had relations with some of the older kids who went to these bonfires. He knew where the spot was and decided he was going to host one. He invited Jon, and I to come to one, as it was going to be our first time attending one of these. It was on a weekend when Jon and I got sent the location. We were told if we didn't have a truck or something that could handle being off-road, we would have to park in a neighborhood and walk the whole way. The place of the bonfire was by the river on the opposite side of the road from a few neighborhoods. Jon and I parked my car by the curb in the nearest neighborhood and started heading towards the spot. We kept getting sent directions to follow a trail all the way back until we saw him and his friends. Jon and I entered the first entrance to the river that was directly on the edge of the main road. With the moon lighting our way, we made our way walking through the half mile of off-roading trails. I could see the distant glow from their fire and vague shapes of trucks from across the way. After about 20 minutes of walking, we finally emerged from the darkness and approached the group of people by the fire. I will never forget when we first walked up and saw about three Jeep Wranglers and one of them was playing the song "T-Shirt" by Migos. I thought to myself, dang this is surreal that we're actually here right now. I looked around and saw most of the people there were older and I didn't recognize any of them besides the kid that invited us. Jon and I didn't know what to do besides awkwardly stand there and watch the fire. As our friend added some more wood to the fire, we were standing by a couple guys and their truck. One of them looked over at us and started to make small talk. After we visited for a little bit, he casually said

"You guys want some acid?"

"No thanks man, I'm good" we said as we continued to watch the fire. Jon and I looked at each other like did he just ask that? We didn't stay long as it was getting late and we couldn't be out much longer. After visiting that spot on the river, we reported back to our group suggesting that it could be a place to hang out and start having our own bonfires down there. They soon became one of the biggest aspects in our life and the stories that later came with it are almost beyond comprehension.

In high school, I came across every level of social groups, one group of people that stayed revolving at our school were the party girls who also were in the popular group. From my perspective, it was one of the wildest groups to exist. We would hear all these stories about them partying, drinking, doing drugs, and doing a little bit more than just cheerleading for the football team. It was a crazy environment that we always heard about, but never were a part of. Truman, Jon, and I met a group of five girls that were in the grade below us, that were heavily involved in the party scene. They thought that our group did a lot of thrilling things and knew we were friends with some of their friends. There was one week that became the craziest week of my life up to that point. We were spending the night at each other's house every couple days. On the first day of this crazy week, Truman and I were spending the night at Jon's house. We got a text from a girl we knew, saying she needed a ride back to her house from this house party she was at. The only problem was...it was two in the morning. We knew we wanted to help out, but also knew if we got caught we'd be in deep trouble. Truman and I decided we would go while Jon kept watch on the house. We took one of our cars and pushed it down the road in neutral so no one could hear the car when it started. The place we had to pick her up was about 25 minutes away across town, but we figured we had a few hours to be back home. We showed up at the house and the girl was being escorted by her friend to our car. Truman and I could tell she was heavily intoxicated. Her friend explains to us that she was pretty drunk and obviously couldn't drive back to her house. Truman and I looked at each other in a way of thinking that we didn't expect to be responsible for driving a drunk person home that night. I felt bad because she was so out of it and nowhere near sober. We decided to drive around a little bit on some back roads to try to give her a little time to sober up before getting to the house. I remember thinking if we got pulled over we were screwed to say the least, but I guess it was better than to let this girl be on the road. We drove around for almost an hour, talking to her and listening to music. We dropped her off and made sure she was able to get into her house alright, she had sobered up a little bit by then. We drove back talking about how weird and unexpected that was, but in the end it made for a good story once we made it back to Jon's house.

The next day, one of the girls from the group we had just met, invited Truman, Jon, and I to a huge party that was being thrown at a venue. Without hesitation, we agreed to go to this party. This would be our first "party" we were invited to, but it turned out not to be what we thought it was. We showed up at the place at around 9 pm or 10 pm. We quickly noticed that this party looked like it was at this small event center, due to all the cars and the people walking into it. We parked the car and walked in. I noticed immediately it was a formal setup event with a front desk person and the bouncer standing at the front. Five dollars later, we were granted entry. The rap music was practically shaking the building as we three walked through the doors into the smoke-filled room. Crazy lights were going everywhere, smoke machines, and at least 100 people. I didn't know what to do since I didn't see anyone there I knew. We just stood in one place towards the back of the room almost the entire time we were there. We didn't recognize anyone there at first until we saw one of the girls we knew emerge from the crowd near the stage. She came over for a brief moment to say hi to us, then disappeared back into the crowd. I couldn't help but think I should be doing something other than standing there with my hands in my pockets. I should've jumped in the center of the crowd and started enjoying the party with everyone, but at this time I was very timid and unwilling to step out of my comfort zone. It was soon after, we all agreed we were bored after being there for about 30 minutes and not doing anything. I gave the peace sign to the bouncer and we were on our way home.

The next day, I spent the night at Jon's house and the group of girls also happened to be spending the night somewhere. Jon and I were watching a movie in his basement when they unexpectedly texted us if we wanted to hangout and drive around, once again it was very late into the night. All these girls were extremely attractive and out of our league, which made us fall into the temptation of agreeing to this. To me, I thought this was a chance to prove that we weren't total nerds to these girls. Sixteen-year-old me thought if we took the chance at hanging out with them this late, they would find us more attractive. Since we had done this once before, it was a borderline routine. We pushed my car down the road in neutral and up a small hill. I even had Jon get out of the car and cover his hand over the exhaust so it wasn't immensely loud when I started it. The girls sent us their location to a neighborhood not far from us. As we were driving up, five of them came running out of the house with blankets and gas station drinks. I was thrown off as they came rushing into the car laughing and chattering. Something we still joke about today, is that one of the girls asked me if she could sit on my lap while I drove, my in-the-moment thinking quickly responded to her with "No I can't because it would be difficult for me to drive." After that night I got a hard time from my friends for not taking up on that offer and I definitely regretted not letting one of the hottest girls at our school sit on my lap as we drove around. You win some and you lose some. The girls told us they had no particular destination, they just wanted to drive around and be out of the house. It wasn't 20 minutes into driving that I began to smell the faint scent of alcohol coming from one of their drinks. I thought to myself, I've been here before, I can do this again. We drove around blasting music and singing along as we all were dancing like we had the whole day ahead of us. We later stopped by a taco place in the drive-through and I couldn't help but laugh when the girls rolled down the window and were screaming what they wanted to the poor guy taking the order. After being out for about an hour or two, we dropped them off and I made my way back to Jon's house. Once we got back to the house, I wanted to make sure that they didn't leave any trash in my back seats. All was looking good until I noticed a shimmer from a glass bottle tucked under the front seat. I picked it up and it was a freshly emptied 1 liter bottle of raspberry vodka. I didn't even know they had this when they first got in my car, it had to be hidden in one of their blankets. I told Jon there was no way this was staying in my car any longer, we drove around until we found a trash can to pitch it in. We reminisced on how wild this night was along with the previous ones, but after not having much sleep these past few days, chauffeuring girls around, and attempting to face some of my disconformities, I was ready to get some sleep.

Another time we spent hanging with this group of girls was when it was a similar situation from before, but not as late from what I remember. Jon and I picked them up from one of their houses and drove around for a little bit. Driving in circles listening to music gets boring after a while so I had to get creative. We couldn't go to our houses, I didn't want to go eat, I didn't want to spend money, so what's the next best thing? The houses under construction. I didn't want to take them to THE under construction house because I didn't want that spot to be well known, I improvised by suggesting we explore a house a few houses down. I had been in this house before so I knew we could get in and I wouldn't look stupid trying to find a random house that were open. We showed up to the house and they followed us into the house, out of all the friends we took to these under construction houses, this was the first time I had seen someone jump up on the kitchen counter as soon as we entered. "Look how cool this is!" One of the girls shouted. I had to remind them that we couldn't necessarily be loud or attract attention, though I often thought that these houses would be a perfect place to throw a giant party, given the right conditions. We went through and explored more of the house and kept an eye on everyone to make sure they didn't break anything. We went upstairs and I sat on a paint bucket while we all stood and hung out in this room. I remember how painfully awkward it was just sitting there and not knowing what to talk about. I remember looking at Jon, thinking the easy part was getting them to hang out with us, but once we did, I didn't know what to do past that. We all were on our phones most of the time, every once in a while one of the girls would say something and I would give a bland answer like "yeah, cool, really?, nice." I won't deny, a couple of the girls had a lot more confidence than me and it almost intimidated me from coming up with sentences to continue a conversation. After we got bored of standing around in that room for a bit, I decided it was time to drop them back off. After I dropped the last girl at her house, I told Jon what I was thinking while I was sitting on that paint bucket.

"Man I just don't know what to say half the time, I get nervous on what to do and it's just awkward sometimes, you know?"

Jon responded with words of empathy, as if we were in the same boat about the situation. At the end of the day, we followed through with hanging out with them all those times, we just had to work on our talking skills a bit more.

8

Working Man

I decided to piece my Sophomore year into two chapters two due to the extensive length. I also happened to get my first Job during the second semester of my Sophomore year. This Job left me with tons of stories and crazy experiences, that I figured I'd dedicate a whole chapter to, then continue back to my last months as a Sophomore. Getting a job early on was important to me, I wanted to be able to say when I got older that my first job was when I was 16. I also like money and enjoy spending it on the things I love, as most people do. I like to think I'm a responsible person and think it's helpful for a young person to get a job early on. A job perfects social skills and teaches how a business works, let alone allows one to manage money and practice time management. I knew I wanted a job, but I didn't know where to start. One of my friends in my math class said he worked at this car wash, and he could get me a job there if I wanted, of course I did! and I pursued his offer. I had just got my license a few months back and was ready to rock-n-roll my way into cleaning cars at minimum wage. I showed up at this car wash a few days later to see if I could get an application, there I met the front desk girl, a few employees, and my soon to be manager. He greeted me with a friendly smile and gave me the application to fill out. A couple days later and some paperwork filled out, I got handed a shirt that literally only said "Car Wash" and I was officially a working man at a car wash.

What better way to get into a first job, than in the summer. It was always hot, scorching hot. Since I was outside all day, the only time I got air conditioning was when I was moving customer cars about 20 feet. The tan was nice, but I wouldn't say it was worth it. I had to teach myself how to do almost everything and learn the process of how the business flowed. There was minimal structure on how I was taught to do my job. One of the employees was assigned to explain what my duties were at this base position. A car would drive up to the side of the building and would sound off the ding of a bell. Someone would approach the car with a type of menu that the customer could look through and tell us what kind of car wash they wanted. From there we would then vacuum the car then take it through the car wash tunnel. For the people up front, they would dry off the car and make the tires all shiny before the customer left. It was a common debate among coworkers whether we preferred working in the front or the back. The back was known as the easier of the two because all one had to do was take an order, vacuum the car, and send it through the wash. The front was a lot more hands-on, drying every last drop of water off a car after it came out from the tunnel. The front was also responsible for washing all the towels, refilling spray bottles, and other small jobs.

My coworkers were the best part. I wasn't aware at the beginning, but I came to an assumption that this business accepted applicants who had fairly extreme criminal records, like it was an opportunity to give them a chance at having a job. Needless to say, the turnover rate at this place was fairly high, but I had many of my coworkers tell me their wild stories. One guy had the most mind-blowing story and the most crazy face tattoos I had seen there. For months I noticed he had this ankle monitor on, but I never bothered to ask what it was for. On one non-busy day, another coworker and I were talking with him and the opportunity came where it wasn't rude of me to ask why he had it. I looked up at his tattoo-covered face and said "why do you have that ankle monitor?" He began to explain to me how at one time he was smuggling mass amounts of drugs and guns into a federal prison and he got caught. It just blew me away to hear that because I could never imagine getting caught up in something like that and here I am, working with a person who has. He then went on to explain how he was doing a lot better for himself working there and getting his life straight. I had one guy try to explain to me that contrails were by the government to drop chemicals on people to get them to think differently. There also was one guy who explained to me how he almost robbed a bank with his girlfriend, but the girlfriend found some extra money in their house so they didn't need to anymore. Every person that worked there had a unique story regardless if they had been in legal trouble. It was like I was in a movie with a bunch of characters that had these distinct personalities. Out of around 15 people total, there were ones that were chill, wise, oblivious, angry, passionate, nerdy, happy, and quiet. There also was an extremely kind, quiet older guy who just kept to himself the whole day, this was Rusty. Rusty was one of my favorite guys that worked there, even though he didn't say much. He wasn't one to smile a whole lot, but when he did, it sure made me feel good. He mainly worked in the back, spraying the pre-soak on the cars before they entered the wash tunnel. Every couple of weeks he and I would have to wash out the sludge, dirt, and whatever else had drained off from all the cars that went out from the center runoff drain. We had to lift up the center grates, then grab six-foot metal poles and swirl them around in an effort to clear the sludge from blocking the drainage pipe. The smell was horrific, I was convinced that if I ever were to swim in that stuff I'd catch every disease imaginable. Rusty was a great guy to work with and I bet this would make him happy if he knew he was a part of a book.

Aside from the wide range of interesting people I worked with, I got to drive some astonishing cars. Sometimes a couple of nicely modified Mustangs, Camaros, BMWs, and Mercedes would come through. One Camaro I came across was chrome vinyl wrapped with huge chrome wheels and butterfly doors. Then there was one time I got to drive a Rolls Royce Ghost, which was extremely cool to experience, with its glowing interior pieces and chrome trim everywhere. Along with driving the wide range of cars, came interacting with an even wider range of people. I took hundreds of orders and talked to many people about what type of car wash they were looking for, many of them still not knowing after I would explain it all. I don't blame them, it was a bit confusing. There were tons of great people I met who came through the car wash, like old ladies, retired dads, and humble businessmen. If they were nice to me and gave me a sense of respect, I would always be overly nice right back and help them with anything they needed. As it was expected, not everyone was so nice when they wanted their car washed. A common trend I began to see was that the majority of people in the high-end cars had a bit of an attitude like they were entitled to a higher standard of wash based on the car they drove. Unfortunately, I had to be the one to explain what kind of wash they wanted to pay for is what they got. Many times I felt like the company punching bag after dealing with numerous unruly people that didn't like how the business was set up. One story I'll never forget is on a blistering hot day there was this guy with his young kid in a brand new lifted truck. The truck was immaculate and the guy who told us to clean it especially well, we always took that statement with a grain of salt because every car that came through was spotless by the end no matter what. When the truck was presented to him as being finished, he got inside and did a quick look over. Me, my friend, and a couple of other people, were working up front that day. We were in charge of wiping down every door jam, dressing the tires, and cleaning every interior piece near the center console. He got out of the car with a sudden confrontational attitude. He was fairly similar to The Rock's body shape, so when this guy started to get mad I told myself I wasn't going to be the first person sent to the moon from his punch. He complained that there was a stray sock in the cup holder and the truck was still dirty overall. Obviously, no one took responsibility for the sock being there, probably because it was most likely his kids. This man was either blind or had never seen a dirty car in his life because that truck was flawless from top to bottom. He started cursing and screaming at us profusely. I felt bad for the little boy to be standing there listening to his dad talk like this to a group of people who just cleaned his truck. A few people started arguing with him and then he got even more upset and threatened to come back and beat us all up. My friend who was with me goes "Alright go ahead, but you'll be in jail for hitting a 16-year-old!" By this time our managers came out and had a few choice words to say to the angry guy. They told him essentially to leave and never return, sure enough, the rest of the time I was there we never saw him again.

The entire time I worked there I was working insane hours for a sixteen-year-old. Every single day from morning until evening, I was cleaning cars. When I wasn't in school I was working, spring break? Working, summer? Working, even winter break? You already know the answer. I am not kidding when I say that in the middle of December and there was ice everywhere, people wanted their car washed like it was June. I would be outside dressed like an Alaskan native while my hands and feet were on the verge of frostbite and would say "Hi there! What kind of car wash would you like?" Truman was looking for a job and for a short time I got him to work with me at this car wash. One of my favorite memories with him there was during winter break. In the back, where we usually spray cars off before they enter the wash, the water would flood and pool up all on the concrete. During the winter it would all freeze over and act as a giant ice rink. I would show Truman how fun it was to slide all over the ice like it was the winter Olympics on a budget. Us both having great experience with skateboarding, we had solid balance skills while on the ice. We would get a running start from one side of the lot and glide on the ice for about 20 feet. Since there were rarely any cars coming through during this time, this was a common pastime. I didn't quite have the proper shoes to handle a job in the cold, let alone with water getting on them. My daily tennis shoes served me just fine in any other season, except winter. Once enough water got in them, ice would start to form on the outside and in the laces. There was a giant diesel space heater inside the wash tunnel to occasionally keep us warm, at times when my feet got super cold I would put my feet in front of the heater. It looked like a small jet engine with fire shooting out of it. Most of the time it took a while for my feet to feel warm and I would look down and see my shoes were starting to melt. By the end of winter, those shoes looked like they had survived a house fire.

Towards the end of when I worked there, there was an unexpected tragedy. Another kid I worked with there didn't have a ride home one day and as we had just clocked out, he looked at me and said

"Hey man, can I get a ride home?"

"Of course dude, no problem," I replied.

I hadn't talked to this guy much while he worked there because he was there for a short time, but I had no problem giving him a ride home that day. About a week later, a few of us at work were wondering where this kid was because he had stopped showing up. Our managers gathered us up in the wash tunnel and told us he was shot and killed in a drug deal gone wrong, it was later publicly released on the news. The workplace was quiet for a little bit after that. It was surreal knowing I had just given this kid a ride and now I would never see him again.

Towards the end of me working at this car wash, I knew exactly how the whole business operated. This job taught me countless life lessons and exposed me to some interesting characters. The people

I got to meet at this car wash will be hard to replicate. It came a time where I was worn out on cleaning cars every day and all day. My manager thought I was kidding at first when I told him I wanted to quit, but he understood that I was burnt out from working there and knew I was ready to move on. He told me "You are the hardest working employee I've ever had and you're welcome a job back here anytime." If that was true or not, I've still never forgotten that statement and I occasionally passed by that car wash to see how things were looking, months after I was gone.

9

Last Half of Being a Wise Fool

After Truman, Jon, and I had a wild month of February and March, April was finally here. School would be getting out soon and all I had to deal with was my math and English class. I took an outdoor adventuring class that semester where half the time the teacher attempted to teach us boy scout knots and the other half was us doing whatever we wanted. Since this class was based in the gym, I knew that Brayden was next door in the recreational basketball class. I would go over and shoot hoops with him the rest of class. In my TSI class, I was getting better at working on computers and I was starting to become better friends with Dawn after her getting to know me better and telling her stories about my friends. Our friend group also met a few new people that would soon start hanging out with us during school and into summer. We have some great stories with these guys so I wanted to mention the time frame when we met them.

We first met Garrett who was introduced to us by Truman, then we met Ty who had a sweet-looking white Mustang, then we met Carson who had an all-black Scion FRS, last, and last there was Braden, who was a guy with a nice BMW, we had kind of known before, but he started hanging out with us more often. They were into cars as well and would start coming with us to the Tuesday car meets and the Memorial car meets on the weekends. Every single weekend we would try to go to the Memorial races and check out all the cars. Truman was friends with a guy from another school that had a super modified candy apple red Mustang Foxbody. It was numbingly loud, but I loved it. This kid drove this car like it was unbreakable. We would watch him pull out of Sonic and he would rev up the engine real high, then drop it in first or second gear and take off. One time he offered Truman, Jon, and I if we wanted a ride and obviously we said yes! We piled in the little red coupe with Truman up front and Jon and I in the back. I guess I underestimated how fast that car was because I didn't think it was going to be anything special, but as soon as we turned a corner with a straightaway in front, it was full blast. He revved the car up then TAKEOFF! It was like we were a red rocket ship flying down the road and being in a 90's car doing well over triple digits was quite the experience. Jon and I were basically holding each other as we continued to blast down the road. I was having a ton of fun, the car was loud, fast, and after a little bit, I started to trust his driving. We came to a stoplight at one point and he turned to us and said

"You guys want me to do a burnout?"

"Hell yeah!" we replied.

The engine roared once again and I heard the tires break loose. With the car standing completely still, we started to look around and a huge cloud of smoke was appearing all around the car. We had done small burnouts before, but this kid was trying to block out the sun. We were laughing extremely hard as we could hardly get over how awesome this was. He took us back to the Sonic and we got out and were all numb from that crazy, but fantastic ride. We also met a girl one other weekend who had an awesome S13 Silvia coupe drift car with a purple glitter paint finish. She had her dog with her and guess what its name was...Silvia. I couldn't help but googly eye her car and express my appreciation for it. She was very humble and told us she was involved in the local drift scene. She asked if we wanted to ride in the car with her up and down the road. Truman was sitting up front, Jon and I sitting in the back, and this girl's dog was sitting in her lap. The noises from this car were magical. I had never been in a car with an RB20 motor before and this brought an abundance of joy to me. Her car was decently fast as we gave it a little juice from 1st gear through 3rd gear in front of the Sonic. There was a small lot about half a mile up the road that was a common place for people to turn around to go back up the strip. We pulled into the lot and she clutch kicked the car into a drift, doing a couple of contained donuts in this small space as her dog was acting like it was just another day. We all couldn't help but laugh in excitement, this girl definitely knew how to drive and her car was perfectly made for it.

By this time during the year, we were hanging at Truman's house every single day after school. As soon as we got out of class, most of us would all drive straight to Truman's and hang out for hours. We'd sprawl out on the floor and couch after a long day at school and either watch episodes of *Top Gear* or *Trailer Park Boys*. Sometimes we just sat and talked about the latest news going on at school and how we enjoyed not having drama like some of the girls we knew. We also joked about the kids who always wore "Drug-free" shirts to school, but then saw videos of them drinking, smoking, and partying. I was content that I lived a transparent lifestyle in what I portrayed in school and out of it. From my view, it was in my best interest to not do something stupid to be then talked about for the next three weeks at school, but some kids wanted that.

A lot of us started to go downtown more often and there was a day when Jackson and I did some exploring. A few years ago in school, we briefly toured a secret underground tunnel that connected a couple of the buildings. There's a story about two wealthy oil families that lived in the above buildings during the roaring twenties. It's an 80-foot tunnel that was built by miners in the late 1920s to connect the two towers. Since they lived in one of the skyscrapers, it made for a useful way to commute through this underground passageway in between the two buildings. It was later opened to the public...if you knew how to get to it. We figured out what building it was, took the elevator down and into the lower levels of the building. There was a way to weave down the old stairs and down some hallways that can get a bit confusing. I could start to recognize where the tunnel was, around the corner of a vending machine, there stood a vault-style door. There was a switch on the outside that gave power to a few lights throughout the whole tunnel. It was a neat place to visit and a great place to take pictures. I remember looking at the interior makeup of the tunnel and thinking that this had been here a while.

As you can probably infer, my friend group had expanded from the original four of us, that was The Hot Sauce Pack. The group of people that we had grown to be great friends with and hung out regularly now included: Jon, Truman, Garrett, Ty, Brody, Spencer, Brayden, Braden, Rogers, Charlie, Zach, Carson, and Me. That may sound like a lot of people to be close friends with, but trust me I had more faith in this friend group than any group at our school. I still was still great friends with Jackson, but he had another friend group outside of ours. At the time, popular trends and lingo were being discovered to refer to girls and guys acting out for the opposite sex. One of the terms was "Thot" or "Begone thot!" similar to the word "Hoe" which more or less refers to a girl who doesn't care about her self-image and only seeks sexual benefits, not worthy of a relationship or respect. Sometimes they would use their looks and charm to manipulate a person for personal gain and don't think girls were the only ones doing this! There were plenty of guys who played this role as well, acting like they were boyfriend material, then later revealing they were only talking to a girl for one reason. It was a harsh reality that no one was willing to admit outside of jokes, but we all knew it was true. Memes were circulating about a "Thot Patrol" being imaginary law enforcement to those who acted like "Thots" and not condoning those behaviors. It was a funny phrase and meaning so we decided to call our group "Tulsa Thot Police" or more commonly referred to as TTP. We now had a name for our group that now became our signature.

Before we started having actual bonfires, some of us would go down there to walk around and explore the area. Since we had never been there much, it was interesting to see what all was in the area and get a feel for where the trails led. There were all sorts of dropped-off furniture, clothes, and random car parts scattered around the sand all over the river area. We later named it "The beach spot" because even though it was a place by the river, the majority of it was a giant stretch of sand. This place brought a great amount of peace and joy to almost everyone who visited it. If you were to see the beach spot, you wouldn't guess there was a whole neighborhood and city just on the other side of the forest. Sometimes I would take Jon there after we got food and would sit in the sand and watch the water go by. May rolled around and we were almost ready to start having bonfires all summer long. The first official bonfire we had was May 5th 2017, Garrett borrowed his dad's truck and we rode down to the river in it. There was a ton of spare wood laying all around the area, so all we needed was some lighter fluid, a lighter and it was time for a fire. It was approaching sunset and we piled the wood up, lit the fire, and found a few tires nearby to sit on. After a short time of this fire going, we met a few guys that came by that were also hanging out at the river. They joined our fire for a little bit as they sat down and talked with us for a bit about where they went to school and so on. A week later, we tried to have another fire, though what was interesting about this one was that there already was a decent-sized fire with a lot of people down there. We joined in on the fire and noticed there were a lot of people, at least 50 that were from different schools. We talked to a few people, but mostly we just stayed with our group and hung out around the fire, enjoying the smokey air. The next day we headed down the river again, this time Brayden mentioned that he had an old Chevy work truck that he could bring down to the beach spot, because two trucks are always better than one. We had another fire that night in a different spot from the night before. We also did more exploring around the beach spot while I rode in the bed of Brayden's truck. We came across a small contained dirt area, Brayden and I almost came up with the idea at the same time of doing donuts in this small dirt area. Brayden floored the truck and out went the back end, I was holding my ground fairly well as Brayden's truck was carving circles in the dirt. We headed back to where the rest of everyone was at and had our fire later that night. The bonfire stories go much deeper than those few stories and I'll go into much further detail later in this book.

Truman got a new truck that was an older GMC Sierra with a Chevy front end. I loved this truck dearly, it had a loud Y pipe exhaust, bigger wheels, and subwoofers that shook the car. This truck is what made me grow a bigger appreciation for V8 engines, after hearing it roar underneath the trees we drove under. The truck may have been old, but Truman loved it and so did we. We even got it stuck down at the river one day but managed to get it out after maneuvering it around a bunch. One day after school we were supposed to be studying for finals but Truman, Brody, and I spent the afternoon installing new tail lights on Truman's truck. We also stopped by the store to get some RC cars to play with. Sophomore year was wrapping up and finals were looking at us in the eyes. I've never been a huge studier and I'm on the verge of not even taking notes for anything I learn about. All my life, when it comes to finals, I simply go off what I remember from the year and hope for the best. I tried out one year studying for hours for my finals and it didn't make a difference from my previous tests. Finals have never been a huge complication in my school life because I know at the end of the day it doesn't matter that much in the whole scheme of school. I've done very good and I've done very bad and there is little difference in my grade at the end of the year. While I was sitting there in Truman's driveway watching my RC car drift all around the driveway and the faint noise of a power drill in the background, I could care less about what my results on the finals were going to be. This is also when Mountain Dew and ramen noodle night was invented; after we went inside later that day Truman fixed up enough ramen noodles to feed a small country and gave us all Mountain Dew sodas, this became a well-known meal on occasion. My 17th birthday rolled around and all I wanted was to hang out at the beach spot with my friends and have a fire, so that's exactly what we did. A couple days later, a few of us were hanging out at the parking garage one night. I was there with Jon, Truman, Brody, and Braden. Braden was telling us how he recently got some Japanese soda from the mall and was curious on how it was going to taste. He happened to have some in his car and attempted to open it. The bottle type he had was the kind where there's a ball at the top that requires a bit of force to pop open, where the ball then falls in this hourglass shape in the bottle. He already had a bit of trouble getting the ball to pop and that was funny to watch, he drank a little bit of it then proceeded to shake the bottle above his mouth, trying to get any of the soda out. The drink went everywhere and as he continued to shake the bottle, he overhand threw it across the parking garage and the bottle shattered into a million pieces. I was laughing so hard looking at all the glass and pop everywhere. This by far was the funniest moment at the parking garage.

About a week later, a few of us visited Truman's lake house for his birthday. Since I had been on his off-road vehicles before I was so excited to do it all again and spend some time away from the city. We spent most of the day riding four-wheelers and touring the area. There were a couple of sharp turns on some of the gravel trails and us being huge fans of drifting, couldn't help but slide the vehicles sideways on the turns. Occasionally doing donuts, exploring more trails that Truman knew, and making funny noises at the cows in the pastures. It was the following night that made the best story of the trip; we were heading down some trails near the lakeside and these trails were on the edge of a forest. This edge of the forest also backed up to a cliff, so the trails were on this cliff that overlooked the late. It was as dark as could be, but we luckily had headlights. Truman took us to the spot that had a great view of a cliff that overlooked the lake. As we turned the motors off, we hung out at this spot for a little bit and enjoyed the great view. Right before we left, we noticed there was a boat with dim lights cruising in the middle of the lake. We didn't think much of it at first, but then the boat started to head towards us, like he saw us. I go "Uh Truman, I think that boat is heading this way." We waited a little bit to see what would happen then a bright flash of light emerged from the boat. It was a spotlight that was quickly turned on and shined right at us. We all started freaking out thinking it was some kind of boat police that were after us. We all hopped on the four-wheelers immediately and were blazing through the trails as fast as we could to go back to the house. The next day we visited the same spot and reminisced on the wild event that some random boat drove towards us and shined his light. We couldn't quite determine what it was, whether it actually was the boat police or some guy just messing with us. This summer would be an awesome one, I had more experience driving so I felt more confident going to new places and seeing new things. Most of the summer included working a whole lot, midnight Taco Bell runs with Truman and Jon, bonfires, fishing, and tons of exploring. I became addicted to finding new spots and discovering hidden places around town. It felt so thrilling to me that not many people either knew about these places or didn't take the time to visit them. One place that Truman, Jon, I discovered for the first time was an underground bridge spot downtown. The interesting aspect about this spot was that it was under an old Route 66 bridge that was blocked off from cars. We had seen other people visit it and from word-of-mouth we knew where to go. To get to the spot, we had to climb the small fence on the side, walk down to the road a bit until we found the open manhole. There was this built-in metal ladder that we took down to where the actual spot was. I turned around after I got off the ladder and saw some junk and random blankets on the walkway. I'm not sure what this place was but there was a sizable platform underneath this bridge that I could walk a few feet on. The scary part about this spot was that it was one jump away from being in the river. It was about a 10x5 feet wooden platform that if you looked down, there was the Arkansas River about 30 feet below. It was weird to think that if I really wanted to, I could jump into the river from where we were standing. Another place we discovered was called "The abandon highway," which was quite literally an abandoned stretch of highway that used to be an interstate about 30 years prior. Brayden told us he knew about this spot, so one day after school he took us to it. Brayden, Carson, Ty, Truman, Garrett, and I all drove out there one afternoon. Since this was our first time visiting, we just spent the time exploring what all was there and having fun driving on this unofficial stretch of road. A few people used it as a pretend drag strip to race against each other or an ideal place to attempt some donuts. Three days later, some of us came back to the abandoned highway. This time it was Jon, Ty, Me, and some friends from our school. Ty's Mustang was the king at doing donuts at this place. Jon and I would stay in my car on the side of the road and watch as he did countless donuts. I rode with Ty a few times as we did several donuts with pieces of tire and smoke going everywhere. The friends we knew from school were there with their friends that I wasn't too familiar with. I was able to meet them and they turned out to be friendly people, we even got invited to pile into one of the guy's Jeep and hotbox it. That became a huge trend in our age group at the time to have "box mods" and "vape sticks" that produced these large clouds of vaporized juice that were sometimes used to "hotbox" cars. About 10 people piled into this guy's small SUV, while Jon and I were towards the trunk with a few other people. In about 10 minutes of a few people smoking their vapes, the car was filled with smoke. The thick white cloud was so dense, I could barely see Jon who was no more than a foot in front of me. We were all laughing because it looked like someone had plugged in a smoke machine in this car. After a little bit of talking and laughing in the back of the Jeep, we all opened the doors at once and the smoke piled out of the car. It looked like the car had fire extinguishers spraying out of it. Soon after this we all headed home, but I told myself I'd never forget about this spot because it was an interesting place to visit.

One thing I did that summer that I definitely wouldn't have expected doing was jumping off limestone excavation cranes. Along the river there was a limestone excavation site that had these huge crane-looking structures with conveyor belts that transported dirt and sand into these enormous piles. I called them cranes, because they looked similar to cranes and it was easy to call them that. It had always intrigued me to go and climb on them someday, so one night I suggested the idea to Ty and Monaghan if they wanted to come with me to explore that place. They agreed and we headed off one night to explore it. We parked in the neighborhood across the street and had to sneakily run across the field, hop a fence, and dodge the light poles to not be seen. The cranes were much bigger than they looked from the street. I would say close to 50-feet or more. These huge dirt and sand piles we're almost the height of these cranes, so I knew if I wanted to jump off it, it wasn't too much of a danger. I made my way around to the base of the crane, where I could walk on the side railing all the way to the top. I slowly made my way to the top of the structure as the ground was getting further and further away. Feeling the crackling paint on the metal railing and my sinking weight on the thin metal on the walkway below me. Once I made it to the top of the crane, it was a surreal feeling of being on top of the world. The houses looked small, cars were small, everything was small. There were only three ways to get down from where I was at, I could either walk back down the railing, scoot my way down the conveyor belt (which was comically fun), or jump off the crane into the dirt and walk my way down from there. Jumping off seemed like the more thrilling option because when would I ever have the opportunity to jump off a 50-foot crane into a giant dirt pyramid? Right now. I had Ty film me as I front flipped into the dirt about 15-feet below me. I was fairly convinced that I could jump from just about any height and be cushioned by the dirt and sand, but I didn't want to push the limits. After we climbed up there a few more times and saw the great view, we eventually headed home. Sneaking back across the field, this time with dirt and sand all inside my shoes. We didn't go back there too many times as it was undoubtedly on the more riskier side all around, compared to our other spots.

It was time to celebrate our country's independence, on the fourth of July of course. Before this year, I had never had an official fourth of July party with all of the guys in the group. A town next door held their annual firework show that displayed on a bridge over the river. Coincidentally enough, one of the better places to view the fireworks was on top of the parking garage we always hung out on. After we watched the parking garage show, we would have our own firework party somewhere else. I dressed up as a dad in his 60's to really get in the mood of celebrating the fourth. Dressed in shorts, white socks with sandals, and an American flag button-up. We all met at the parking garage along with many other people who were also there to watch the firework show. Night came and we sat there on the hood of our cars watching the fireworks light up the sky as I drank my Mountain Dew "Dew S A" flavor. It became one of my favorite Mountain Dew flavors but it was sold only for a limited time. The firework show concluded and we headed to our spot to light our fireworks. We went to an empty parking lot in the back of this church that was up the road. One of the guys said he had some illegal fireworks that were well over the limit of what our city allowed without a permit. We were going to light that one last because after we lit it, it was time to scram. We lit a few small fountains, sparklers, and firecrackers then went to light some roman candles. We talked about how funny it would be if we had a full-on roman candle war and have an all-out battle with these sticks. Braden, being funny, lit a roman candle in each hand, ripped off his shirt, and started screaming like a barbaric madman, firing the candles in the sky.

We all played along like he was firing at all of us as we ducked for cover as he continued jumping and screaming with balls of colored fire soaring through the air. It was totally spontaneous of him and I got a good laugh from that. Then it was big illegal firework time. After we cleaned up most of our trash, it was time to light the big one. One of the guys got the firework out of his trunk and it was a box that was the size of four car batteries. He put it out in the middle of the parking lot far away from our cars, in case anything went wrong. We all agreed that once the firework went off, we would get the heck out of there! I stood on standby near my car as I watched him lean down to ignite the fuse. Once the sparks started I knew there was no going back and the whole neighborhood next to us was about to hear every second of it. It shot up like a normal firework then BOOM! a huge flash of the gigantic explosion of colors and light, lit up the sky for a moment. It was extremely loud and I felt the ground shake when it went off. I remember scrambling to get in my car as I was laughing in disbelief at how loud and big it was. As we flooded out of the parking lot, ash was falling from the sky onto our cars. Our firework show definitely ended in a bang.

There's a story from that summer that involved Truman's truck, a thunderstorm, and my bladder that I'll never forget. I was with Truman, Jon, our friend Emily and we were heading to drop Emily off at her house after hanging out one night. We were all in Truman's truck and it was pouring rain so hard I thought the sky was going to run out of water. She lived on the opposite side of town than us, therefore it was a bit of a drive to get to her house. I told Truman that soon I was going to need to take a trip to the little boy's room. We got to about a mile from her house, when I told Truman the gates of the dam were moments from opening. He suggested the idea of dropping me off at this park a few blocks away from her neighborhood, then he would come pick me up on his way back. Keep in mind it was still an absolute downpour outside, but I was in full agreement with him. He pulled into this park, drove towards the back, and let me out as I'm trying my best to open the door without getting a lot of rain inside. That was one of the most satisfying times going to the bathroom in my life. Standing under a tree as it's pouring rain, thundering, lightning, and I'm just having a grand old time. It wasn't long after when I heard Truman's roaring exhaust through the competing noise of the thunderstorm. I hopped in the truck probably looking as if I had also taken a shower while I was there, but nonetheless we dropped our friend off and my bladder could live to see another day.

The last great memory I have from Truman's truck is the time when Truman went to break up with a girlfriend. It was a funny situation where about half our group gathered down the street from this girl's house. We planned to pile into Truman's truck bed, while Truman drove up to say his goodbye with all of us hidden in the back. It had just finished raining so I was glad we didn't have to wear ponchos for this top-secret mission. Before we left the meet-up spot, I remember rapping the song "Rap God" by Eminem in Garrett's car. We all piled into the back of the truck a few blocks down, then once we were all settled, we showed up at her house. He parked on the curb and went up to her porch. None of us could hear anything they were saying, but we were trying so hard not to burst out laughing because she had no idea a group of guys were casually in the back of his truck. As soon as Truman got back to the car and started to drive off, we all popped up from the bed and let go of the most erupting laughs. I had never done anything like that, but I'm so glad to have been a part of it.

One of the final stories from this summer comes from a day that I honestly didn't know if it would happen or not, but thankfully it did. Remember that girl I had a giant crush on that I met during winter break? She lived kind of far so we didn't get to hang out, but she said we would someday? Yeah, today was this day. We had vaguely made plans that I would pick her up one afternoon and bring her back to my town where there was more to do and see, plus I was excited to show her some of the spots I had recently discovered. Prior to this, I had never driven so far to hang out with a girl, but I'd say it was worth it. I set out on the highway blasting music with the windows down and I was beyond excited to finally be able to see her, let alone hang out. I parked in this small town that I had never been to, this is where I would pick her and her friend up from. I remember looking around at the old buildings around me thinking, I can't believe I actually made the journey to come here and see this town that I had never been to before. After a little bit of me twiddling my thumbs in the car waiting for her, I see an old truck pull up right next to me. I look over and see a girl about my age, but it wasn't Zoe, so it must've been her friend. Sure enough, I see Zoe pop up from behind her friend in the truck. I couldn't believe she was actually here. She and her friend got out of the truck and into my car. With big smiles, we said hello to each other and I got to meet Zoe's friend Courtney. I was right, she was a million times more gorgeous in person than she already was. It was surreal to experience something I was so excited about, then for her to be right in front of me. I can't even put into words how unbelievably stunning she was, I couldn't help but smile every time I looked at those soul-piercing blue eyes and radiating shine from her blonde hair. I'm trying to put into perspective how dreamlike of an experience this was for 17 year old me. It was easy to make conversation with her, even though it should've been the opposite from my previous experiences. Her friend was also kind and lively which lightened the mood and made me feel comfortable. We got back into town and I took her to an ice cream shop. Half of the reason I did this was so I could occupy myself with something while I talked to her, so I wasn't as nervous. From there, I took her to a few places I wanted her to see, the first being a spot I haven't mentioned yet, but I frequently visited. Jackson, Jon, and I found out about this spot during mid Sophomore year. It was an easy access spot to the river by a trail from a dead-end road. We first discovered this spot on a class trip during science class one day. The name refers to an old rusty boat that's beached on the shore that sits across from the Jimmy Buffett casino on the other side of the river, giving it the name "The SS Buffett." We hung out there for a little bit just talking and walking along the rocks. Then of course, I had to take her to the legendary parking garage, which wasn't more than five minutes away. I actually happened to run into Truman and one other friend of mine who was also hanging out on the top. We all talked for a bit and enjoyed the view of a beautiful Oklahoma sunset. I said my goodbyes to Truman and we left the parking garage as were close to heading home. I told her that Jon wanted to say hello, which he did, but really I just wanted to show Jon I had achieved the goal of getting the chance to hang out with Zoe. We showed up to Jon's house as they also got met in person for the first time. After we left Jon's house, it was time to hit the road. It was well into the night by the time we got back to their truck. We said our goodbyes as I told them I had a great time getting to drive them around Tulsa for an evening. I then began my drive back to the homeland with the utmost feeling of happiness and satisfaction.

10

Monkey Business

The summer going into Junior year was filled with excitement. Every year I made it a goal to have a better summer than the last. It was fairly similar to the ones previous, except our group hung out a lot more and visited new spots more often, like the parking garage, beach spot, downtown, and other smaller spots. The under-construction house was no longer under construction and we drove by it one day and saw someone had finally moved in, little did they know. Zach had purchased a used Ford Ranger after the Golf was getting its second or third transmission replaced. This little truck was awesome, it had a different feel compared to Truman's truck because it was small and compact. Zach and I were driving around finding off-road spots and fields to drive in. Even though it had factory wheels, stock suspension, and 2-wheel drive, it still handled most everything we threw at it. There were a few fields and hills Zach knew of that were behind the highway, we would go out for hours and drive around up the hills and in the dirt. One of the hills had a great ramp structure to jump, while I got out and filmed, Zach would hit this ramp going about 30mph and jump the Ranger on the top of this hill. One day while we were down there driving around, Zach drove into an area where there was tall grass. All was going well until we drove through one section and heard a loud pop, we realized he had accidentally hit a concrete storm drain that was hidden in the grass. We pulled out of the field and took a look at the wheel to see that it was clearly damaged. One phone call later, his dad showed up to pick us up and the Ranger would have an appointment with a new front tire to off-road another day.

Taking pictures has always been an underlying hobby of mine that I haven't thought about until then. I took many pictures with my phone, but never questioned the idea of getting a more professional camera to use. I had saved up money from the car wash and was ready to get an actual photography camera, the Canon 60D. This is one of the more budget-friendly cameras but still has great quality. This was my first step into the journey of photography and a tool to allow me to explore the realm of taking pictures even further. I figured since I like cars and photography, I would combine them. I then made the Instagram page: "NextGearDown," where I would get to display all of my pictures of cars I had photographed. I enjoyed taking pictures of other things at times, but cars were my main subject. I've been a huge fan of the sport of drifting my whole life. When I got older I always dreamed about going to these drift events and maybe even owning my own drift car one day. Around the same time that school started that year, a drift event was being held near the capital of Oklahoma. A few people from TTP and I attended this drift event. All the awesome cars that I had seen on Instagram and in movies were now right in front of me, everything from 240s, an S15, Supras, and RX-7s. One aspect I was excited about is that I would be able to take pictures of all these legendary cars. I believe this was the first-ever drift event we ever went to and it was one to remember. The track was a decent size and the cars had no hesitation giving it their all. Engines screaming and smoke filling the sky, clashing in perfect harmony. We were there all the way up until dark, but it almost made the cars look cooler as they drifted under the lights with smoke shading the cars while they continued throughout the track.

I was full-time back in school, luckily I was halfway done with the entirety of high school, which at the time I didn't know if it was a bad thing or a good thing. I had gotten most of my harder classes out of the way that I needed in order to graduate so the majority of the reminder classes were fairly straightforward. This year is when I had my first homecoming dance, I purposely didn't go to the homecoming from the previous year because I thought it was silly, but once I warmed up to the idea of it I was excited to go. I didn't even know what homecoming meant, all I knew is that it was a dance that we could go to during the school year and it's traditional. I didn't have a date that year, I just went with our group and some friends. For some reason, I also wanted to dress up like a rapper, with big diamond chains, glasses, and a grill. "Clout goggles" were trendy glasses at the time and those paired with the diamond-filled grill would be the centerpiece to my outfit. When I first went to get my jewelry, I walked up to one of the jewelry guys at the mall who was sitting on his phone and probably was waiting for the day to be over. I asked for his help in finding me a grill with a bunch of diamonds in it. Obviously everything is fake diamonds and fake gold, but it looks like a million bucks and that's all I needed. I picked out my grill and a couple of big chains. On the day of the dance, we met up at a local spot we had previously known of that was a lake on the outskirts of town. We took a bunch of pictures on the dock and the gravel road. Spencer was able to come down for homecoming and he also was with us to take pictures at the lake. In some of the pictures, you can see us wearing the clout goggles and me with my diamond-filled grill. Then it was time to party, the dance was somewhere downtown where traffic couldn't have been any worse. This dance was the least fun out of the ones I went to, but it overall wasn't a bad time. We had a ton of fun, got to meet up with all of our group, take pictures, and listen to some great music while wearing the infamous clout goggles. Once we left, most everyone went home, but I still wanted to burn the rest of the night up. A friend and I heard that there might be a bonfire going on that night at the river. He had a 4-wheel drive truck so it had no trouble going through the dirt and sand. After we changed out of our suits, we headed down to the river at a quarter past midnight. We saw a small fire in the distance, but it didn't look that big. We got closer and saw two guys standing by it with their Jeeps. We pulled up to the fire and got out to say hello. One of the guys was Jack Haines, who I had previously known from TBS back in middle school. His friend Jack Monaghan was with him and that's where I got to meet him for the first time. Since they both were named Jack, I would call them by their last names to not get them mixed up. We stood by the fire and talked for a bit and I mentioned to Haines that I remembered him from TBS and I had no idea that he knew about the beach spot down by the river. I should've expected that since Haines had an older lifted Grand Cherokee and Monaghan had an older lifted Wrangler, which both looked like they could handle anything off-road. From there, both of the Jacks slowly started to meet everyone in the group, including our recently met friend Colby. He had become friends with Jon, Brayden, and Zach, and then began to hang out with all of us. Soon after, Haines also started hanging out with us a bunch. It was either Haines or Colby who told us about this one spot to explore that was being constructed. It was being built to be an indoor soccer facility, but what was unique about this place was that the giant hanger of a building sat on a huge plot of land, I'd say about 10 acres worth. We could see it from the road and there were a few dirt trails by the road that we could follow back to the facility. This whole place was called "Titan." One night Haines, Colby, and a few other friends drove up to Titan, looking to explore it. Since I had previous experience exploring under-construction properties, this was another spot to conquer. It was a vast and open building with gravel dust and dirt coating the floor. The best way to describe it would be to say it was similar to three giant airplane hangers lined up next to each other. There was all sorts of machinery and equipment in there from the workers, we even would play on the scissor lift to raise and lower ourselves. The best part was that there were openings that had more than enough room to fit cars and trucks inside the facility. What some people did was they would drive through the opening, drive all around inside the building, and do donuts in the gravel. It was an awesome place to explore and we said we definitely had to come back to experience the rest of the place.

One night, a few days after we explored Titan, a few of us went to hang out in the parking garage. To our surprise, there was someone up there that we recognized who was also hanging out with some people. There was a kid who was a notorious partier and all-around wild guy. I noticed he was acting kind of funny, but it made a lot more sense when I saw the multiple cases of beer all in the car. There were countless empty beers all in the seat and I know he would've been done for if the police had seen that. Not to mention the amount of risk this was, being at the top of a parking garage and having to go back out the same way he came. At the time it was hilarious because he was screaming and climbing all over the car in a comedic rage. I could tell this probably wasn't the first time he's done that, because after talking to us, mid-sentence he goes "Oh sh*t I gotta get home! See ya!" then slammed the door and sped off down the parking garage and down the road. We all looked at each other like what a weird situation to experience.

School was becoming more enjoyable to go to, not because I had any special classes, but because I had a rhythm to my day. Every morning our group would hang out before school in the parking lot. Since we all parked on the back row of the lot, we didn't have to worry about anyone parking next to us. We always had a great time goofing around before school started, either we would pile into someone's car and listen to music or just stand around and talk. This year I took the same basketball class that Brayden was in and all I had to do was shoot hoops to make a good grade. All my required classes were almost out of the way so I was able to relax throughout the year, even more than I already was. I also was taking TSI for the third year in a row because I was having so much fun in that class between rebuilding computers and talking with my few classmates and the teachers. I became better friends with Dawn and I would tell her some stories about the adventures of me and my friends at bonfires. Then it was off to Algebra 2, where I would ask myself on a daily basis, why did someone come up with mixing numbers and letters together. I don't think I would've passed that class if our homework wasn't for a completion grade. Even when I randomly wrote out equations to make it seem like I knew what it meant, that was barely keeping me afloat. At lunch, I'd either get chicken nuggets or pizza and make my way over where the guys sat. Even in Junior year, I still dreamed that a food fight would break out one day. After school, I'd either go home and play video games or hang out at one of the guys' house, where I could forget about why it was important to multiply fractions.

On a Monday one week, I was giving Jon a ride to school and it happened to be his birthday. We were pumped up for school and ready to get the day started. I pulled out on the highway and got the music going to enjoy some jams for Jon's birthday on the way to school. About halfway there, I was coming around a long corner in the middle lane, then I noticed there was a guy on a motorcycle in front of me. The motorcycle seemed to have started to slow down below the speed limit, since I was behind him, I instinctively slowed down as well. After a closer look I noticed it was a highway patrol motorcycle, right as I noticed this, he swerved into the left lane, slowed way down, got behind me, and pulled me over. This was my first time being pulled over and I would've never thought it would be from the front. I got my information out as my heart rate was slowly increasing as I was quite nervous. The gentleman who pulled me over definitely did not have a good morning and was a little angry to see me. He started off confrontational and explained I was doing well over the speed limit with some sarcastic remarks. I was respectful as one could be as I tried to explain that if I was doing over the limit, then he was also. He then adds that my school parking sticker and air fresheners were an obstruction of view and was a ticketable offense. I explained to him my parking sticker was required to be in that position and I had to have it there. He stormed back to his car as I looked at Jon with a fearful nervous look. The more time that went by, the more I was starting to think we would be late for school. He came back with a scroll of papers that almost went down to his feet. He handed me a mandatory court ticket for speeding and obstruction of view for the parking sticker. Dad was not going to be happy about this one. Even Jon thought I was driving the speed limit, but that didn't change the fact I had court in a month. To no surprise, we were very late to class and I had to explain to my history teacher that I had just got thrown the book.

Some of us heard out about an abandoned National Guard armory that was tucked away in a small town about an hour away. With our craving for more exploration, we dedicated a day on the weekend to check it out. Truman, Jon, and I drove out there and found where exactly it was. Oddly enough this small castle-like structure was sitting in the middle of this neighborhood of this small town. It was all boarded up and chains locking the main entrances. After further inspection, we made our way to the side of the building where there was a small wedge of plywood in one of the windows that we were able to squeeze through. It was kind of scary after we made our way into the building because if for some reason we had to quickly get out of there, it would be an issue. When I first made my way through the wedge and into the building, it was this giant room with a bunch of old dusty stuff everywhere. There were multiple rooms to go into to see the rest of the building. We slowly made our way through the main hallway that led into another big room. There were rows of piled-up stadium seats, chairs, and graffiti on all the walls. It was spooky how old and deteriorated the inside of this building looked, along with the lack of light coming through the windows. One by one, we eventually looked around in most of the rooms, there was even one room that looked like a control room with a bunch of switches and buttons all along the wall. We weren't in there for too long before it started to get dark and trust me, it started to look scary once the sun was going down and we could barely see our way out of there. One after another, we all made it out of the armory, to visit it another day.

We revisited Titan once again and this time we brought more of our friends and more vehicles. It had rained the night before so it was very muddy all over the surrounding land. It sure made for an awesome mudding park as we got in Haines' Jeep and plowed through the ruts with mud flying all over the car. It was a big playground to drive through and throw mud everywhere. At some point in the night, we were outside of the complex, gazing at Jack's Jeep that was caked in mud. We heard a car coming and looked down one of the gravel roads that led up to where we were. We couldn't see anything but a bar of light from a light bar on the front of the car. We weren't expecting anyone else to show up so we immediately thought it was a cop and we scattered in every direction. The forest was my closest escape route and so was it for Truman. We both immediately dove into the forest at full speed, running further into the woods away from Titan. We came across a single mattress in the middle of the wooded area. It was halfway clean and it was brush-free compared to the forest it was in, therefore it looked like not a bad place to lay down and wait until we figured out what to do. We got separated from everyone else so we had to call someone to get information on what to do. It turned out it wasn't a cop but was our good friend Molly in her truck that had a light bar. We didn't expect her to show up and that's why we all freaked out at first. We went back into the Titan building, where we showed our friends the spot and explored the second floor and all the things we could climb on.

In December of this year, I went to my first actual concert I wanted to go to. On December 16th of 2017, Brody and I went to a "$uicide Boy$" concert in downtown OKC. The Suicide Boys are two cousins that were underground rappers. I had been listening to them since freshman year and they were one of my favorite music artists at the time. Even though I didn't quite like the name of their group, I enjoyed their music. One of the main reasons why I fell in love with their music is because for years I grew up listening to mainstream rap and music that everyone listened to. I found one of their songs in a car edit and thought it sounded phenomenal. I then looked up more of their songs and discovered the rest of their discography. Their lyrics were beyond extreme from the basic music I had listened to, they were not only explicit but extremely aggressive and violent. This type of rapping drew me in because they did not cut any corners when it came to being raw and transparent in their writing of music. This also opened me up to the other underground rappers that I quickly got to like such as Bones, Lil Peep, and Night Lovell. Their lyrics are pretty extreme, but I saw through the influencing themes and appreciated the rawness and authenticity of what they were explaining in some of the songs. I respected the $uicide Boy$ wild persona they portrayed in their music and I wanted to experience that live. It was a cold rainy night when Brody and I drove down there. The line was already wrapped around the building by the time we got there, but at least we were there. About an hour went by and we finally made our way into the building, I was so excited I could barely sit still. It was an open venue-style building so we could make our way to the front if we wanted to. Before the show started they began playing songs of other rappers like Pouya, Denzel Curry, and Lil Peep. Then the $uicide Boy$ came out and started their performance. It was incredible, the bass was shaking the building and everyone was singing along to the songs. I probably looked out of place there, with no tattoos and not smoking a joint, but I was still having a great time. This was also the first time that I was in a "mosh pit" which is where the crowd opens up an empty pit in the middle and once the song goes into the main beat, the crowd will clash together and purposely push and shove each other into one another. It was amazing being in a full crowd when a song is at its peak and I was aimlessly running into people. My favorite part of the night was when it was getting close to the end and I was hoping they would play my favorite song from them, that being "LTE," which also was the song that introduced me to them. They tricked us by saying it was the end of the show and they walked off stage. The crowd then began chanting "One more song! One more song!" over and over. They eventually came back out and the crowd went nuts. They then would play a couple more songs before the show actually ended. The first song was none other than "LTE" which I was bouncing off the walls when I first heard the beginning notes. I looked at Brody and said, "I'm going into the middle of the pit for this song!" With no hesitation, I made my way in between everyone and up to the front of the stage. The song was getting ready to go into the main part and I was about to explode in happiness like a bottle rocket. The song started and the crowd went crazy, I gave it my all throwing my arms up and jumping as high as possible. After the last couple of songs, it was finally over. I was sore from dancing and running into people, but I had one of the best experiences in my life. I couldn't have had a better time and I definitely did not expect to be in a mosh pit. The ride home was calm and quiet as we were both exhausted. The ambient lights from the highway accompanied us all the way home.

Similar to Sophomore year hanging at Truman's house, we started hanging at Haines' house every other day after school. Aside from working on his Jeep, Jack loved tinkering and working on small engines. One day we went over to his house and he had recently purchased a small yellow dirt bike that he was going to fix up. It was hilarious as we got to ride that little bike sometimes, putting around the neighborhood. He also had a go-kart frame that was laying around and I happened to have a leftover small motor I used for a small bike I had restored. I gave Jack the motor and that became the heart for his go-kart. Once we got it running and all the parts needed for it to drive properly, we spent an afternoon taking turns driving it around the block. For an old go-kart and a 200cc motor, it had some power behind it. Then we got creative, Jack had a colored smoke bomb that he wanted to tie to the back of the go-kart while someone drove with it on, leaving a trail of smoke behind. Colby got in while Jack tied on the smoke and sent Colby down the road with a blue trail of smoke behind him.

A few days after messing around on the go-kart, it was fall break. On one of the first days Ty, Monaghan, Haines, Jon, and I went and bought girl scout cookies. It was a super nice day out so we headed to the river for a bit to soak in the sun. I remember riding on top of Haines' Jeep eating my box of Tagalongs. Later that night after hanging out at Jack's house the whole day, we went to Memorial and ended the day off by watching the street cars race up and down the road. Also during this break we revisited Titan and for some reason, it happened to be raining again like it was the last time. Though I can't complain too much because rain meant the mud would be a perfect condition to go through in the Jeeps. We drove around a bit more, driving up the small dirt piles and slinging mud everywhere. Spencer also happened to be with us, as he was visiting from out of town. This time back they had completed a bit more of the inside of Titan and there was green turf all on the inside with lights that were on 24/7. I felt like we were in a movie as our whole group was running freely across this giant stretch of turf with no one else there. We got up on the second floor and would run back and forth across the platform. A day or two later it rained all day and drifting is always better in the rain.

In March, some of us got to go to a big drift event that was being held about an hour away. What was different about this drift event, was that they were doing ride-alongs. If I bought a helmet, I would have the chance to ride with one of the drivers. After being there for a couple of hours and taking pictures of the high horsepower cars ripping up the track, I was able to get a ride. I approached the driver of one of my favorite cars at the event and asked if I could ride with him. The driver's name was Ben and he owned a baby blue 240sx S13 with a 1JZ motor, almost the perfect car to me. With no hesitation he said yes and I was about to ride in my first drift car. Roll cage, bodykit, angle kit, and more, it was nothing like I had ridden in before. Truman got to ride in the car behind me and we got to be a part of a tandem, which is where two drift cars will drift the track in close proximity to each other. I strapped up my race harness, put on my helmet, and was ready to rock-n-roll. We didn't even reach the first corner before I had a smile from ear-to-ear. I could hear Truman's car behind us and we flew into corners at about 60mph, going through the gears and pulling the handbrake. Ben was doing an amazing job and it impressed me as a person who's never drifted. We finished the track and I could not stop smiling while telling Ben he did an awesome job. We were there a couple more hours before heading home and going to Memorial to watch more fast cars later that night.

There was a time towards the end of Junior year where I experienced a weird medical situation that changed how I thought about my life forever. I began experiencing weird feelings in my gut. I was at home one night eating my dinner and I gradually started to feel sick. I couldn't finish my meal, I was burning up and I was not feeling good. My stomach started to hurt and I was getting a weird numb feeling. I was freaking out like this was nothing I've ever felt before, it felt like I was having appendicitis and I was not prepared to go through something like that. I decided to try to fall asleep to get through the pain and assess it in the morning. I made it through the night, but my troubles were just beginning.

For the next 2 weeks, I was curled in a ball in my bed with a constant weird feeling in my gut. I would lay on my mom's bed because I had minor PTSD from being in my room from when it first began. I would look at the ceiling and try not to fixate on the weird sensations happening in my gut. Oh God please let me be alright, I told myself often. I felt helpless and unable to get anything done. The feeling was indescribable. I would go to school and constantly have abnormal feelings in my stomach and some days I would go home early because it was too much to bear. I'm a tough person, most things that get thrown at me I can handle fairly well and get through it, but this was a whole different enemy. I missed the last week of school because I could barely walk, good news was that I would miss finals, bad news was that it wasn't going anywhere. There was a huge car meet at the drag strip called "Import Face Off" and I borrowed a wheelchair so I could still go to the meet without having to walk. My family and I decided to get it checked out because it was not going away or had any signs of it. After multiple tests, talking to multiple doctors, and going through my first CT scan, it had been concluded that I had an amount of waste buildup all over in my intestines and could be semi-cured with help of some medicine. The news lifted the dreadful fear off of my shoulders. During the time of my great discomfort and not being able to move for days on end, I thought I had some cancer or something requiring surgery in my gut. From those events, it has made me more of a grateful person than I already am and I'm thankful to function properly every day I wake up. I remember laying in my bathroom hurting and thinking, I take for granted being healthy everyday, I should be doing things everyday to better myself. That experience opened my eyes to be the best person I can be and do all the things I can before I can't, because I knew that feeling at one point.

After school got out and my stomach started to feel better with the medicine, I was up and around again. Haines told me about this traditional party that he and his family go to every year with their friends called the "Crawfish Boil." It was basically a giant cookout with boiled crawfish being the main dish. Jack told me that he would be the cook of the crawfish and was in charge of putting together all the ingredients into the giant bucket to boil. When we showed up they gave us beaded necklaces and glow sticks, topping off my crawfish boil attire. I had never had crawfish before but they look like mini lobsters, so I had to try it. I sat in a lawn chair as I watched Jack dump the ingredients into the pot. Small corn on the cob, potato slices, sausage slices, bits of lemon, and of course the hundreds of crawfish. Right before we put the crawfish in the pot, Jack and I got a couple of them and would watch them sway their claws around. They were even able to hold a small necklace or plastic straws, which was hilarious to watch. When the crawfish were done cooking, Jack lifted out the inner basket in the pot and ran over to the giant table where he would put the food, yelling "The crawfish are done! Time to eat!" Everyone in the backyard ran over like they hadn't eaten in months and began devouring everything on the table. I didn't know if we were supposed to get plates or silverware, hence I just stood there looking lost, then one of the adults came over to me and said, "Just eat it all with your hands." That was fine by me as I inserted my way to the table where I grabbed my first crawfish to eat. Jack could tell I didn't know what to do with it once I got one. He told me the best way to eat a crawfish is to twist off the tail, suck the juice out from the body, break a little off the tail, and bite out the meat. This proved to be the most efficient way to eat crawfish, once I got it down a couple times, I was back to the giant table of food. I found a new appreciation for crawfish after I ate about twenty of them. By the end of the night I was almost full of crawfish and the lights in my glow stick necklace were starting to fade. Seafood always makes me sick if I eat a lot of it, but my first time eating crawfish was a thumbs-up for me. My first experience at a crawfish boil was amazing and I knew it wouldn't be the last.

11

Bonfire Season

During high school, I went to about 100 bonfires total down at the river and each one of them has a story of their own. Some are definitely more wild and crazy than others and those are the ones I want to tell you about. For almost two years straight we had bonfires every weekend or every other weekend. Like I mentioned before, we first discovered the beach spot during Sophomore year and spent a bunch of time down there during that summer. From Junior year and on, is where the bonfires got exciting, and the stories got better. I've got some insane stories from bonfires at the river that I wanted to leave a whole chapter to. To give you an outline of how we did our bonfires and how they went, we would source out wood pallets to pick up behind stores. We would either take Haines' Jeep or our friend Molly's truck and go behind a number of large stores to see if there were a pile of wood pallets in the back. After we loaded them up, we got cans of gasoline or lighter fluid. We would drive down to the beach spot and find a good place to have the fire. There were three spots along the river that were prime bonfire areas. The first one was big and open, but there was deep sand, the second spot was less deep of sand but an overall smaller area, and the third was a small dirt lot that we rarely visited. The first crazy bonfire story of Junior year would later go down in history as one of the most legendary bonfire stories. I've told this story many times and I love re-telling this because it was so thrilling at the time.

It was a regular night of having a bonfire, it was Haines, Monaghan, Braden, our friend Kole, and I. We all got down there and set up the fire and got the music playing. After we were there hanging out by the fire for a couple of hours, we noticed a small light coming towards us, later revealing it was a helicopter as it got closer. Planes and helicopters flew over us all the time, but this one looked like it was headed right towards us. We all thought it was kind of weird at first that this helicopter had gravitated towards us so precisely. It moved above us and it started doing circles above the bonfire. We all thought that it was some rich guy messing with us like it was a private helicopter scoping out the area at night and they happened to come across us having a bonfire. It was kind of funny but at the same time, I didn't know if we should be concerned. Then all of sudden as we kept looking at the helicopter, a giant beam of light shot out from it and lit up the entire bonfire spot. We were all freaking out and screaming in panic, it went from perceiving it as a rich person flying a helicopter to now this was probably the police that was after us for some reason. We all immediately scrambled inside our Jeeps and trucks. Monaghan was freaking out because he'd lost his keys in the sand and couldn't find them right away. He found the keys and it was time to get out of there. I hopped in Kole's truck and we were both freaking out as we tried to get in and put the truck in gear. We abandoned the fire, left all our stuff, and hightailed it out of there. Usually, we would drive slow down to where we would have our bonfires, but this time we were full throttle through the dirt and sand trails out of the river. Both of the Jack Jeeps couldn't go that fast but they could definitely handle the dirt and sand way better than Kole's truck but we still managed to make it through okay. There was an outlet of the beach spot that led onto the main road once we left the river. We were the first car out, so once we got out to the road, we either had to make a right or a left, both are long stretches of road that lead out to the main city. We knew we had to decide fast whether to go left or go right. Keep in mind that the helicopter is still chasing us, after he shined the spotlight on us they did not hesitate to follow us out of the river and onto the road. Right as Kole and I were leaving the river to pull out onto the main road, the helicopter shifted its spotlight onto Haines who's all the way in the back. I don't know why the helicopter focused on him, but we assumed they were identifying the vehicles to the local police. Kole and I decided to go right because there were fewer stoplights and longer stretches of road. As soon as we pulled onto the road, we saw that there was a police car with its lights on, nosed in by one of the entrances to the river. There were few choices to be made on what to do, therefore we flew past this cop car. I don't think he could've chased us because his car was positioned in a way that it would be difficult to go after us. We went down about a half-mile up the road and then we took a sharp left onto this stretch of road to then put the pedal to the metal. I didn't even look at the speedometer, but I can assure you it was definitely not the speed limit. I looked out the window and I could still see this helicopter following, I saw the beam light coming down from the helicopter as it's chasing both of the Jacks out of the river. I then get on the phone with Haines and Monaghan and tell them to meet up in a parking lot so we can regroup. After a little bit, the guys made their way out of the river and some way or another they lost the helicopter. We think the helicopter gave up and or just wanted to get us out of there and scare us. We met up in a grocery store parking lot and we're talking about how wild that encounter was. In retrospect, we ran from a helicopter and flew past a sitting police car, one of the wildest things I've ever done. We later heard that the same police car we saw parked outside of the river entrance was hit by a drunk driver, luckily the officer was not in the car when it happened. The next week at school, I remember telling a few kids in my class about what crazy experience I just had the night before.

Most of the time when we got pallets, they were secured all the way down until we got to our fire. Except this one time where the pallets got revenge on one of our friend's truck. We had this fire that we were looking forward to all week, bringing tons of drinks and snacks. Aside from Haines' Jeep that we loaded with pallets, we also loaded up our friend Kole's truck. Sometimes the trails got a little bumpy heading towards the spot. "Whoops" would take shape in the dirt and would bounce a truck up and down. We may have been going a bit too fast over these whoops with these unsecured pallets because after about four or five big bumps, we heard the back window of this truck shatter. I looked over my shoulder and there was glass everywhere. This wooden pallet was in the backseat of the truck and it was a mess. We got out and could not believe that this pallet had enough force to bust through the back window. The show must go on, we brushed off as much of the glass out of the truck as we could and continued on with the night.

We got creative on the things we would burn at bonfires. As I mentioned earlier, there was all sorts of stuff scattered around the beach spot. One time we found a couple of old tires and got the idea to throw those on the fire. I thought that they would burn normally, but instead the tires tended to burn intensely, shooting black smoke up into the sky. The tires would have strong circulating winds inside the tube of the tire, then when the majority of it was burned, it would start melting with blue and orange fire dripping off the side. One thing that we had to be careful with, was that the black smoke would not dissipate but stick together and carry all throughout the sky. We figured if one were standing in the neighborhoods a couple miles away that they could see the dense cloud of black smoke. It was fascinating to watch a tire being burned, but that probably wasn't great for the environment. Aside from old tires, we burned couches, lounge chairs, umbrellas, car seats, TV's, and hands? Yes, at one point there was a time where a couple of the guys set their hands on fire. There was this trick going around that one could put a layer of alcohol on their hand and the fire would burn off the alcohol, not affecting their hand. Us being boys, we had to try this out. A couple of the guys put the alcohol on their hand and lowered it down to the flaming pallets. Almost instantly, I watched their hands engulf in flames. It didn't go identically to plan as the fire ball on their hand freaked them out, hence we all freaked out watching this as they frantically shoved their hand in the sand. Tree leaves were also amusing to burn, because they wouldn't produce as big of a fire, but the burn pattern of them would be satisfying. A couple times we went down there, there was a giant pile of leaves about 15-feet long. Dry leaves are easy to catch fire so most of the time we didn't even need lighter fluid. Being that leaves were superb at catching fire, when we didn't have gasoline or lighter fluid, we would light a pile of leaves then put our wood on top of them to light it.

In January we had a fire where we burned a couple of huge TVs. My friend's parents were throwing out an older broken 70-inch TV. I asked them if I could have the TV instead of throwing it away, as I saw it as a perfect item to throw in a bonfire. At this bonfire, I invited a couple people from my science class to join in on the burning of this giant TV. We brought food, snacks, and got the music playing. Before we actually threw the TV in the fire, we took turns hitting the screen with an axe. I think destruction of items is beyond satisfying, therefore I had a bunch of fun doing that. After the front of this TV looked like it had been hit by a car, we finally threw it in the fire. It took two people and a decent swing to get it to the center of the fire. Towards the end of the night, we happened to see a big glass box TV that was in the woods, we threw it in the truck and went to put it in the fire. After we laid it down in the fire, on top of the other TV, one of us had the idea of taking the axe and hitting the glass of the TV to see what would happen. We got my friend, who I invited from my science class, to do the honors of hitting the TV. This was his first bonfire he'd ever been to and I doubt that he'll ever forget it. With all of us standing around, he took the axe and gave it one mighty swing to the center of the TV. Within an instant, the TV exploded into a million pieces with the sound of a sonic boom. The blast was so excessive, I had to look around for a second to make sure everyone was still accounted for. We came to the conclusion that the gases from the fire were building inside the TV, which caused it to violently explode once the glass was broken. Even though huge glass chunks from this TV went flying, everyone was okay. The blast's impact was so strong, it blew the blade of the axe off of the handle and we found it lying about 10-feet away from the fire. Friend who hit the TV was not only happy he wasn't hurt, but beyond excited that he did that. He told us that was the craziest thing he'd ever done and we were proud to give him that experience.

One night when we went down to the beach spot to have a fire, there was another big group of kids having a bonfire near one of our spots. We went over to say hi and introduce ourselves. We found out that they were their school's main bonfire group, similar to how we had become. They were super cool guys and had no trouble making friends with us. One aspect I liked about them was that they were a bit more country than us, cowboy boots, cowboy hats, trucks, and a whole lot of chewing tobacco. One kid even showed us his collection of dip cans that were carefully organized in a poker chip case. We came across them a few times during the year while we had bonfires, sometimes we would go to theirs, sometimes they would come to ours. They always brought a lot more people than we would. They would practically bring half of their school on big bonfire nights. We thought we brought a lot of people when 15 or 20 people would come to our fires, this group would bring close to 100 kids when they had big fires.

At the beginning of summer after Junior year, I had the idea of getting a blow-up mattress, a paddle, and sailing out on the river.

This sounded like one of my best ideas yet and I committed to it. I went to Walmart and got a decent size blow-up mattress and a 5-foot rowing paddle. Once we got down to the river, Haines had a small air pump that we used to blow it up with. I drug it out to the sand bar, where I then grabbed my paddle and prepared for take-off. I honestly didn't know how it would work, but I was going to make sure it did. I sat on it and felt the bottom of the water, then I took my paddle and continued to push off the bottom until I drifted out more into the river. Soon I was floating away with nothing but my paddle as we were all laughing as I drifted more towards the center of the river. The current wasn't strong at all and I maintained a slow float the whole time. It was amazing, taking in the euphoric experience of floating on a river on an air mattress with the sun setting in front of me. Some of the other guys wanted a chance to float on the mattress, so I paddled back to shore to let them have a try. One after another, I watch some of the guys climb onto the mattress to aimlessly float on the water. I could tell the mattress was starting to lose air, probably due to all the people getting off and on it a bunch. After we had our fire, I threw the deflated mattress in my car later that night to sail the river another time.

Towards the end of junior year, Jon was talking to me at lunch about how people were starting to talk about our group and our bonfires. Word had gotten around about the helicopter chase and the TV explosion.

"Dude, people are starting to talk about us!" Jon said.

"Really?"

"Yeah, I had one kid in my class, who I've never talked to, said he heard about our bonfires."

"That is awesome!"

I never thought word would spread at school that our group had these bonfires, but it was bound to happen after all the videos and advertisements.

12

The Final Summer

I came to the realization that this was my final summer as a high school student before going into college. Time flies when you're having fun and that couldn't be any more true. With it being the middle of June, the lake adventures were in full swing. Jackson invited Truman, Jon, and I, to the lake. We had visited his lake house one time before and had a great time, but since we were a little older, it was going to be that much better. We had named the lake trips at Jackson's lake, "Lakeside," this being the second trip, it was called "Lakeside Vol. 2." On arrival Jackson mentioned one of the small fridges was stuffed with all the Arizona tea we could drink. The next day would be where the fun really began. I woke up the next morning to "I'm Upset" by Drake being blasted from the speakers downstairs. I walked down the hall, looked off the upstairs railing, and saw all the guys dancing around downstairs. We had all just woken up, but that didn't mean we couldn't blast rap music at 10 in the morning. It wasn't soon after when it was time to head out on the water. Once Jackson's dad got to the house, we were able to head out on the boat to go tube, swim, and everything in between. We started off tubing for a few hours. The tube we were being pulled on was a two-seater, hence two of us went tubing at a time while someone would be on the boat filming the people on the tube. I knew my dad was decent at throwing me around a tube, but Jackson's dad was a different animal. He knew the perfect methods to get us to hit the biggest waves and sharpest turns. He would go in circles a few times, get the waves gigantic and choppy, then go full speed, dragging us through the waves. My arms would cramp up from holding on the tube handles. There were a couple times where Jon and I got sent flying into the air after we hit a six-foot wave or so. The Landing was the worst part because there was little to no cushion on the tube when we slammed down on the water. Even though I enjoyed tubing, I equally enjoyed watching people ride the tube. I could see the upcoming waves as they got closer and would be sent into the air, either successfully landing or getting tossed in the water. One of my favorite places we visited was called "Dripping Springs" which was a marina, Yacht club, and cliff jumping spot, all in one. There were a number of boats with a bunch of college kids, probably doing the same thing as us, enjoying the summer break. I didn't jump off the big cliff the last time I was there, but I was more than determined this time. There are three cliffs at this spot, the small one, which was about five feet, the 15-foot medium one, and the big one that was around 45-feet. Jackson was a seasoned veteran when it came to cliff jumping at this spot. With no hesitation, he made his way all the way up to the top, tossed the life jacket at the bottom, and jumped in. Jackson explained to us the reason he tossed the life jacket down at the bottom, it's to disrupt the water and visualize where to land. After being there for about 20 minutes, swimming in the water and watching Jackson jump off the cliffs, I figured it was time to give the big one a try. I climbed up to the top with Jackson as I stepped carefully on the rocks leading to the cliffside. The longer I was up there, the longer I began to realize how high up I was. The worst thing I could have done was look around and see how small everything was, I did exactly that. Looking down wasn't that bad because I could understand what 45-feet was, but the fact that these houses and trees nearby were the size of my finger was terrifying. I was just sitting up there taking everything in, like there were only two ways down, walking or jumping. In a way, it reminded me of jumping off that excavation crane. I watched Jackson jump with ease as his feet left the rocks as I saw him disappear off the edge and into the water. I knew I was next, but I didn't want to face it. I scooted a little closer to the edge, trying to mentally prepare for this. I realized that it was 90% mental and 10% physical, as many things are. All I had to do was jump and make sure my body was straight with my feet pointed down, it was getting myself to do it was the hard part. Jackson gave me great words of advice to try to follow, don't think too much about it and just jump. Extremely easier said than done, but he's right. After I tried to understand what that meant, I no longer began looking at the house, not focusing on how far the drop was, I just had to jump. There were even some other people down at the bottom in their boats cheering me on and saying I could do it. After I tossed down my life jacket, that was the point where I thought I couldn't back out from. I got a small running start to clear the rocks and I jumped. In the milliseconds of me leaving the cliff I thought, wow I actually just jumped off this. It was the definition of a freefall as it felt like I got close to terminal velocity. I was in the air for a second or two before crashing in the water below. The pressures and force that came down on the water, once I landed, were incredible. After I popped up from the water and realized I wasn't dead, I thought holy crap, I just did that and it wasn't bad at all! Instantly proving I was worrying for nothing and I just had to commit. After the first time, it was as if I had been jumping off that cliff for years. I climbed back up and with no thought, I jumped off of it again, again, again. Though it does get tiring after climbing up those rocks a bunch and hitting the water that hard. Jon was able to jump also, but he learned from me and knew you can't stay up there long and think about it, you just have to jump. He tossed his life jacket as it slowly fell into the water. He wasn't up there long before plummeting into the water. He popped up out of the water and had a look of discomfort on his face, we swam over and he told us he landed a little bit leaned back and the water smacked him pretty good. That's the only part that can be tricky about jumping from this cliff, the landing has to be near perfect. After being at Dripping Springs a bit more and jumping from the other cliffs, we wrapped up being there and went to other parts of the lake.

On the second-to-last night after we got in from the water, Jackson wanted to fix us a five star gourmet meal, Dino Nuggets. Who knew that the most basic form of frozen food was secretly the pinnacle of lakeside dining? To accommodate this tasty dinner, he suggested we listen to the song "Dinosaurs" by Blake Rules, which is a rap song about dinosaurs made for little kids. He played this on the big speakers as we all danced around watching Jackson pour the dino nuggets on the oven tray. 15 minutes later, they were done as we danced around the oven like it was a native ritual. We had the song on repeat as we continued to dance and sing-along while eating the dino nuggets. We went out to the back deck where I noticed one of most breathtaking sunsets I've ever seen. I could not explain the amount of blue, pink, orange, and red that were perfectly woven in this Oklahoma sky. The orange and pink haze from the sky surrounded us as Jackson brought out the second batch of dino nuggets. We ended the night off by watching the movie "The Secret Life of Walter Mitty." The feeling of being at the lake and watching Walter Mitty longboard across the windy roads of Iceland, couldn't make me any more happy.

The following morning, I was woken up by Truman tossing a shoe on me. I tend to be a heavy sleeper, therefore I was the last one awake. The day went about the same as the ones before, tubing, cliff jumping, and getting sunburned. I suffered a minor tragedy that day while on the tube. I went to toss Jackson my sunglasses in the boat so they wouldn't fly off. I thought the throw was adequate but instead I watched them hit the side of the boat and into the water. Just like that, one of my favorite sunglasses was now at the bottom of the lake. One of the funnier moments I remember while on the water was that we decided to check out an island on the lake. We all got out of the boat and a couple of us had floppy hats, I turned to the guys and acted like I was a Navy Seal encroaching on the enemies on the island. They all went along with it as we played along like we were army guys with guns, trudging through the water, about to investigate the island. Later that evening on the water, we took time to park in the middle of the lake and listen to music as the sun began to set. Jackson knows a lot of great songs through his vast taste in music. As the sun sunk below the water and the stars started to reveal themselves, we sat in silence around the boat and listened to "Sedona" by Houndmouth and I loved the part where it went "I remember when your neon used to burn so bright and pink, SO BRIGHT AND PINK!" Another one of my favorites was "Space Song" by Beach House. This song later became popular, but I was glad to first hear it out on the lake before many people knew about it. The song has this euphoric dream-like melody and it was as if I was aimlessly floating on top of the water looking at the stars. I almost merged my consciousness with the peaceful environment of the song and the night sky. One of the last songs we listened to was "I Am California" by John Craigie. We all really enjoyed this song and it was the perfect way to end a night out on the water. We said our goodbyes to the wonderful place at the lake and set sail for the journey back home.

Our whole group wanted to take some kind of summer trip that wasn't too far away. What better place to venture than the great state of Arkansas, particularly Fayetteville. About a week after we got back from the lake, we set out to the home of the Razorbacks. Our first stop was a state park about an hour away called "Natural Falls." As stated in the name, the main attraction is a waterfall in between a ravine in the park. Once we got there, we walked the trails to the bottom of the waterfall, at the bottom was a viewing area where we strung up our hammocks all along it. About five or six hammocks were hung on the platform as we listened to music and watched the waterfall for a bit. It was a tad humid, but it was nice to lay in the hammock and listen to the water crashing below. Our next stop was a restaurant in Fayetteville called "JJ's Live" or "JBGB," a burger place and brewery. Once we got there, I realized that not only was it a restaurant, but a whole playground. Out front there was a sand volleyball court, ring toss, corn hole, and a pool. By the way the outside looked, I knew it was going to be amazing food. They happened to also have "Cards Against Humanity," which is a hilarious card game we enjoyed playing together. We played that while waiting for our food and I nearly laughed myself out of my chair by the end of the game. The food was unbelievable, I got a burger with fries and a drink that seduced my taste buds. I remember Charlie got a whole plate of Catfish bites that looked so mouth-watering, it made me rethink what I ordered. We then concluded our meal and went outside the restaurant to check out all the activities. I didn't come prepared to swim but Zach and a couple of others did. We hung outside of the restaurant listening to music, while Zach and the others hung out in the pool. After JJs, we headed into the main part of the town of Fayetteville. It was blistering hot that day and I was itching to get in the AC. We visited a couple pawn shops and got to see the left behind treasures that were in some of these places. Something I thought was interesting was that I saw a Nintendo DS for $30, I thought back to when I had one and that cost me seven times as much. We started the voyage home after walking through a few more shops. On the way home my stomach started to hurt a little bit, more towards my appendix area. I didn't think much of it as I tended to have discomfort in that area quite often, though it started to bother me after it never went away. By the end of the ride I was begging Truman to drop me off first, but we were closer to Zach's house, making it inefficient to double back around. I stuck it out until we got to my house. I was convinced I was having appendicitis and was waiting to go to the hospital, but after a little bit the pain started to go away oddly enough. I couldn't believe it, all through that miserable ride home and it just goes away? I'll count my blessings I guess.

Fourth of July came around once again and this time there was a much bigger group of us. By this time, some of the people in the group either moved away or stopped hanging out with us. We're still friends with some of them, but time goes on and things change. We had learned from last year not to go to the congested parking garage, especially with our large group. We heard about a place by our high school baseball field that had a great view of the town's firework show and that's where we went. We first met up at Zach's house where his family was having a Fourth of July party. Zach's house was also where we would return after the firework show to shoot our fireworks. We had some food and hung out at Zach's house before heading to the baseball field. The guys in their Jeeps drove over the curb and into the field by a giant tree, where we would claim our spot for the night. We met up with a couple of our other friends that came to watch the fireworks with us. Most of us brought our hammocks and we strung them all in the trees and in between all the Jeeps. Before the fireworks started, I saw that one of Zach's friends brought his girlfriend and she was definitely on the cute side. I whispered over to Zach "dang, his girlfriend is really cute." I guess Zach told his friend what I had commented. Zach's friend was a defensive linebacker for his football team, about six foot five, close to three hundred pounds, walked over to me and said,

"What'd you say about my girlfriend?" I immediately went into submissive mode, no way was I fighting my way out of this one.

"I just said she was cute, I'm not trying to do anything, I'm a wimp dude, you have nothing to worry about." I wanted to say everything to make him think there was no chance of me interfering with him and his girl. He immediately lightened up and said it was no problem. After I escaped being crushed like a soda can, I looked at Zach and went "Seriously dude, did you really have to tell him that?" He kind of laughed like he knew what would happen, then it made me laugh. The firework show started with bright explosions of color illuminating the sky. Some of the guys brought girls to swing with them in their hammocks while they watched the fireworks. I was by myself in my hammock, but it would've been nice if I wasn't. After the forty minutes of fireworks concluded, we drove back to Zach's house to light our fireworks. Brayden brought a lot of big fireworks, Haines brought a ton of Roman Candles, and the rest of us brought other small stuff. There's a field across the street from Zach's house that was perfect for lighting fireworks. We all would place the fireworks in the center of the field and run back towards the street when they were lit. We shot off some erupting ones that shot up in the sky, others were either firecrackers or smoke bombs that we would throw in the water drains. It was funny to watch Haines toss firecrackers by people's feet to make them jump before it went off. Overall it was an awesome time spending the fourth with all my buds and we would do it all again next year.

The rest of the summer we all went hammocking almost every single day. Jackson was one of the first people to introduce hammocking to Jon, Truman, and I, and we passed that hobby on to the rest of our group. Hammocking is simple, yet so fun. We would find a spot nearby, either at a park or a playground at a school and would string our hammocks in all sorts of directions while listening to music. The best part is when we would get food and eat it while in the hammock, a prime eating spot. Getting into the world of hammocks was exciting, like what kind do it get? A one person or two? What kind of straps and clips do I need? I got one of the name brand ones, as most of us did, with a bigger surface area, heavy duty carabiners, and straps that can support up to four hundred pounds. I love my hammock and I took it just about anywhere we went all around town.

A couple weeks later I went on a trip to Branson, Missouri with my family for a week. About half way there, we stopped at a hotel that happened to be near where Spencer lived. I texted Spencer and said I was close to him and he happened to drop by the hotel to hang out for a bit. I wasn't doing anything with my family that day, so after a little bit of hanging at the hotel, we went back to his house and played video games. I always thought that it was funny that I unexpectedly got to hang out with Spencer on this trip. Once we got to Branson, we visited Silver Dollar City and rode a bunch of rides on the main strip of Branson. Mini Golf and go-kart riding are always my favorite, it always gives me a chance to tunnel-in my inner race car driver. After I got back from the Branson trip, Spencer coincidentally enough, came back to visit our group for a few days. We tried to do as much as we could during the time Spencer came to visit. On the first day, we spent hanging out at Haines' house; then later that evening, we visited the same lake we took our homecoming pictures at, Lake Bixhoma. All of us brought hammocks and we strung them up side-by-side along the dock on the water. Jon turned on the Bluetooth speaker and we hung out swinging in our hammocks with the sun setting across the water. At one point during the evening, we got curious on what temperature the water was, surprisingly it was fairly warm. Spencer contemplated if he should hop in the lake just for the heck of it. Of course we all wanted to see him do this and so he did, he got up on the railing of the dock and jumped in.

Two days later, after Spencer headed home, we went on a float trip. This was a trip we had planned to raft down a part of a river. A couple of the guys had been on a float trip before and they knew the best spot to go. This float trip would turn out to be legendary to look back on and I can't wait to get into what all happened. We headed off to the rafting place that was about an hour away, singing and jamming out to music all the way there. At one point during the drive, when we were close to the location, Brayden climbed outside of the window of Zach's car and got on his belly while holding onto the front two doors. We were laughing hysterically as we continued down the road with Brayden laying on top of Zach's car, until he climbed back in. Once we got there, we were greeted by all the staff members who briefly gave us the rundown about how it was going to go. Since we had a big group, we would take two of the large rafts with us. We loaded up our bus, which would take us to the raft spot, with all of the stuff we brought. Somehow, a cooler full of "apple juice," made its way onto our bus. The older bus driver guy even suspected it would and he joked that as long as all of us were accounted for by the end of the river, he didn't care. I was so excited, I had never been on a float trip before and I love anything to do with water activities. We arrived at the starting point where I saw the rafts we would take with us. We all drug the two six-person rafts out onto the shallow bank of the water. At 11am we had seven miles of river ahead of us and no rush to get there. Once Zach got his Bluetooth speaker going and we got settled in our rafts, we were ready for the day. There we were, floating down a river in a raft with all my best friends. There were a few checkpoints of popular spots that either had rope swings, a decent swim spot, or cliff spot. We only had to use the paddles to steer or get out of shallow spots, other than that, the river would slowly carry us down the way. Our first spot was two rope swing places, right before the first mile mark. On one side was a regular rope swing on a tree and on the opposite side was a small rope swing with a slippery mud runway that people could slide off into the water. I first visited the lone rope swing, because I had never been on one before. I wasn't experienced enough to do the flips off of them, but I still had fun gaining momentum on the swing and flying off. Then I swam my way against the current over to the other side. There were a few kids sliding off the mud slide and that looked super fun. Colby and a few others joined me as we took turns getting a running head start and penguin-sliding in the mud and off into the river. At one point, Colby landed wrong after he went off the mud drop-off and landed on some sort of rock, taking a quarter-size chunk out of his shoulder. Shortly after the river took a bite out of Colby, we headed down to the next spot. We approached a slight right curve, where on the left was a huge drop-off cliff that looked like I could jump off of. There was a shallow bank across from the cliff that allowed us to park the rafts while some of us got out to jump off the cliff. I first went out to where I would land after jumping to make sure the water was deep enough for me to jump in. Sure enough it was fine and up I went to jump. It was a steep face off terrain I had to climb up to get where I needed to go to jump off this cliff. After reaching the top, I walked through a small path that led to the runup for the cliff. Charlie, Zach, and Brayden came with me to jump off of this. One of the guys went first as I got to witness how they landed, how deep they went, and what the water did. This all gave me information on how I was going to perfect my jump. I got a running start and off the 15-foot cliff, I went soaring in the air. Since I had some experience from Jackson's lake, I was quite comfortable jumping from this height and higher, I just had to make sure to land right. Once I jumped a few times normally, I wanted to step it up a notch by attempting to front flip off of it. When jumping off various heights of cliffs into the water, especially flipping, I tend to build a sense of how long it takes to reach the water. Adding a rotation, compared to simply jumping, could add or subtract that time. Doing a slowed front flip can help me judge how fast I reach the water on most every jump. After I tried a front flip and got down the timing, I began to flip off this cliff more comfortably. Once we had our fill of this spot, it was on down the river we went. It then started to get cloudy, the sun wasn't as harsh and a wave of cooler air moved in. We hit a shallow spot on the river that was unavoidable. To prevent the bottom of the raft scratching, we all got out and pushed the raft across the thin layer of water above the rocks. I felt like we were in military training because it took so much of our combined strength to push this giant raft through the shallow part of the river. We came across a couple more spots to jump off of. Once we got close, I hopped out of the raft, jumped off the cliff, and swam back to the rafts. About a mile or two before we reached the end, up ahead there was a section of rapids that were off a small drop off in the water. We got all excited as we settled down in the raft to brace for impact as we went over the water. It was like a scene in a pirate movie where we were about to crash into the biggest wave of the ocean. Once we hit the rapids, the bottom of the raft began vibrating tremendously and we all jokingly got scared and started screaming. It wasn't that bad, but it was funny pretending like it was. The end of our float was near, I could see a checkpoint where the people ahead of us were dropping off their rafts. I then proceeded to chug a root beer and front flipped off the side of my raft. Surprisingly I didn't throw up after that, but I almost did once I saw some of the guys pouring the apple juice down their back and the others tried drinking what was left that was running off of them. What a float trip this was. We started approaching the end, where we met back up with our bus driver who would help us hoist the raft out of the water and into the trailer. The water was much colder in that part of the river, so it was almost perfect timing to get out. We got back on the bus where my body was worn out and I could feel the sunburning developing on my back. There was a wasp flying around on our way back to our car and I thought if that sucker stung me, that bus driver would hear some creative vocabulary. We got back to the cars and loaded up all of our stuff out of the bus and into the cars. We then headed back to town an hour or two into the evening with river water stained in our skin. Later that night we went to an arcade that Brayden worked at, he was able to get us in for "free.99" anytime and let us play all the games and activities in the place. Almost every weekend during Junior year we would go to this arcade and play the games. After the float trip, we went bowling at this arcade. One of us had the idea that it would be funny if someone threw a bowling ball up to the ceiling. Brayden was up to bowl and accepted the challenge, with one big swing, Brayden delayed the release time of the bowling ball so it skimmed the ceiling above and it crashed down onto the bowling lane. We all were rolling in the booth seats laughing so hard after the ball smacked down on the wood. Even after a couple of days after the float trip, we still talked about how enjoyable it was and how we wanted to do it again.

I wanted new wheels for my car. Little did I know, I made this much harder on myself in the long run, but that's the pain of learning. I bought Truman's old wheels that were still in great condition. They were silver wheels from Hyundai Genesis Spec-R. I got tires put on them soon after the float trip, and it was more expensive than I was expecting. I kept them silver for a few weeks, but I eventually wanted to paint them gloss black. I did so much research on how to correctly paint wheels with spray cans, because I didn't have the resources to do it professionally. The temperature had to be a certain humidity for the paint to have the right curing condition and in Oklahoma that proved to be quite hard. I hand sanded each wheel, prepped them with primer, and painted the first layer. When I went to do the second layer, the paint started bubbling and peeling. I later researched on why this happened, even though I had relatively good humidity levels. There were many reasons that can cause this to happen and I may have gotten all of them. Painting these wheels was a battle I never thought that would last longer than it did.

Another drift event came around and this time it was at a track in the capital of Oklahoma. It was cloudy the entire day but still felt like a desert. I never got to ride along with anyone because I forgot my helmet, but it was still amusing to watch and take pictures. Towards the end of the event, the people hosting the event offered to anyone that they could race their car on the track for one lap for free. Truman told me he wanted to race his car, so I hopped in the passenger seat and we got in line. Truman's car couldn't drift because it was front wheel drive but he instead used the track like an autocross course, full traction and sharp cornering. We got up to go on the track and they waved us a green flag. He floored it going into turn 1 and prepared for the second. From all of our crazy driving experiences, Truman knew how to drive a car pretty well. By the time we got to the end, we both thought it would have been an impressive lap time for what his car was. It was getting scorching hot by the time we were leaving OKC. We stopped by McDonalds on the way back and that air condition couldn't have felt any better.

In the last week of July, some of us went out to Truman's lake house for the weekend. The two days were jam packed full of adventures from everything between exploring the small neighborhoods around the lake to talking about life on the back porch at midnight. The first day we spent riding around on the four wheelers and golf cart, exploring more trails and dirt roads. Later that night, we parked our four wheelers on the beach and had a small bonfire from gathering together small logs. It was awesome sitting there watching the fire with nothing but my friends and the moon. The next day was fairly similar as we drifted down more trails and had deep life conversations with cows in a field. I noticed the rain clouds above started to form a bit throughout the day, but I didn't think much of it. We visited a small beach on one side of the lake on our four wheelers. There were a group of boats, seadoos, and tons of people. We parked our rides and hung out at this beach for a little bit while talking to the dad's on their boat about enjoying their weekend. From there, we went further down the lake through more trails that Truman wanted us to explore. I noticed the storm clouds were looking a little darker than they were earlier and we started to hear thunder in the distance. About five minutes later from this observation, I felt a raindrop and then another one a few seconds later. We were about a mile or two deep in a forest on the edge of the lake that was only accessible through trails. Once I felt this raindrop, I hoped it wouldn't be too bad, but I was very wrong. Within five minutes from the first raindrop, the rain started pouring. I had to squint my eyes a bit more because the rain was increasing in density within the forest. It was in that instant that Truman rallied us together like we were about to crusade on enemy forces. Yelling over the heavy rain and erupting thunder, he said "Just follow me and we'll get out of here!" It was a full-on thunderstorm with heavy rain, mud flying everywhere, and cracking thunder above us. I don't think I had been out in this heavy rain before in my life, the raindrops hurt as we flew through this forest getting pelted with rain. Truman was in front, Zach was second, and Jon was riding with me in the back. All I had to do was see where Truman or Zach went on the trail so I knew where to follow. Every few seconds we would hear the loudest snap of a lightning strike close by. We didn't hold back on the gas, it was full throttle going through this forest. We were all screaming from the combination of not being able to see clearly along with the rain feeling like we were getting hit with paintballs. It was one of the most chaotic events I've ever been in, frantically trying to make it out of the forest, on the lake, in a thunderstorm, a mile away from the house. We got to a place where I began to recognize the trails that were near the house. I saw Truman take a turn out of the forest and onto the dirt road that led up to the house. Zach and I followed right after him and we soon pulled into the driveway. We were all soaking wet, I just prayed my phone wasn't fried after that wild ride. Somehow it was fine and we all made it inside the house safely. It rained the rest of the day, but I was glad that we made it out of there fine.

13

Beginning of the End

The last summer of high school was over and I came to the realization that this was truly my last year in grade school before going to college. Upon that realization, it made me harness the mindset that this would be my best year of high school yet. I was now at the top of the food chain I once feared, I was now finishing up my final months in federal priso- I mean the education system. I had gotten all my hard classes out of the way, and I was riding the Senior wave out until the end. I took weight training, TSI, food prep, computer programming, and history through film. I made it a mission to make my Senior year as easy as the first day of preschool. By this time everyone knew what their place was in school, meaning everyone stuck to their social class and rarely broke their mold. I knew a couple people trying to go out with a bang from who they were from the previous three years, by either dying their hair, getting tattoos, or dressing crazy. I even tried switching things up by pushing my hair to the opposite side it had been for the last 18 years. I also had become much more independent and wore exactly what I wanted to wear. I also didn't have anyone to sit with at the lunch table that year, so I would get my food and eat it in the backseat of my car. Eating chicken nuggets, laying on my backpack, and listening to music. I was living my senior year like I was newly retired from work, enjoying my time with few responsibilities.

A week into school our group was acting like it was still summer and I was perfectly okay with that. Me and a few of the guys, spent a night exploring more of downtown and seeing what spots we were able to climb up on. Though we had to be careful because a week prior, Truman, Jon, and I were exploring downtown and I pulled down a giant ladder on the side of the building and the alarm went off. We went down some alleyways and saw more of what was behind these giant skyscrapers. We came across a fountain in the central part of downtown. It was on some sort of timer where all the water on the fountain would stop for about 15 seconds before starting up again. A fun game we would play was that when the fountain would stop we would see how many times we could run through it before it turned back on. It was a very intense game because sometimes the timer would be longer or shorter when the water came back on. Zach and I ran through it a few times, until Zach got hit with some water. He was only in shorts and a t-shirt, hence he decided it would be more fun if he just ran through the fountain while it was at peak spray. We were all laughing hysterically as Zach looked like he had spent the day at a waterpark after going through this fountain several times. We ended the night off by driving up and down the streets of downtown, while Jon and I were hanging out the window singing "What About Love?" by Heart.

We continued going to the Tuesday car meets and the memorial races every weekend. Everyday felt like Friday because our group would hang at Haines' or Truman's house after school, then go to car meets, go to the arcade, or some adventure that involved a crazy story. It was like everyday was something new. At school, the campus police knew our group quite well because we had gotten busted from doing burnouts, drifts, and revving our cars in the parking lot. For example, Haines and Charlie were taking turns drifting in the parking lot before school after it had rained. Jack had recently purchased a 240sx, which is one of the best drift platforms money can buy, and it was the perfect conditions to test out what it could do. Most of the time we were alertful about looking out for cops nearby before people would drift but this time they came out of nowhere. They saw Jack and Charlie mid-drift in the parking lot. I was sitting in my car with Jon as we watched the patrol car swoop in the parking lot and flash his lights. After a little slap on the wrist, we were able to laugh about it and go on with the day. I also had my fair share of encounters with our campus police. During senior year, I had my car searched three different times. What's funny is that I knew people who graduated without getting their car searched once. I don't know if someone was trying to get me in trouble or my car begged for unwanted attention. Multiple times I was pulled from my classroom to accompany a search on my car. On the third time I was searched, my principal and the drug man escorted me out to my car to conduct a search. While the dog attempted to smell something, my principal said

"Are you nervous?"

"No," I said with an affirmed tone.

"Are you sure you're not nervous?"

"No I'm not because I know there's nothing in there."

I was getting irritated because I knew this was a waste of time. The drug guy dug around my car a bit more until he came across a multitool. He showed it to my principal and asked why I had it. I explained that my dad gave it to me for my birthday in case I was in an accident and needed to cut my seatbelt. He then exited my car and told my principal that he couldn't find anything else. In the three times I was searched that year, they found nothing and I knew they wouldn't.

The amount of bonfires slowed down because a lot of our group had sold their Jeeps and trucks, but they weren't completely gone. Instead of every weekend having a bonfire, it was closer to every three weeks. Every year we went to the big football games throughout the year, some being at nicer stadiums. Zach was one of the guys who would run our team's flags across the field when we scored. Zach said one of the flag runners was gone and Haines volunteered to substitute with no problem. We didn't know if he was allowed to, but we knew it would be hilarious. The next time our team scored, Jack jumped down from the stands and grabbed one of the flags in the back. We were all screaming and laughing as Haines scrambled to pick up a flag and followed Zach and the other guys across the field. It was priceless seeing all the flag runners with body paint with our team colors, then here came Jack in a regular t-shirt and shorts. Later after the game, we met up at a movie theatre parking lot and hung out while Zach went through multiple water bottles, trying to get his body paint off.

A couple weeks into school, a few of us went on a trip to Dallas for a couple days. Formula Drift Texas was on the schedule that week and there was no way we were going to miss it. We had purposely missed the first day because it was qualifying, therefore we had a full day of the actual event ahead of us. I rented a high quality camera lens to bring on this trip so I could get some extra professional shots of the cars drifting. I was busy going to car meets and preoccupied with other activities, thus I forgot to pick up the lens the day before we left. I had never been so furious at myself that I was never getting that rental money back for a lens that I never would use. I had brought all my other lenses and camera gear, therefore I was not completely out of luck. I had never been to Texas before this trip and I was pumped up. Charlie, Truman, Brody, and I drove down there Saturday morning and one of our first stops in the lone star state was a Buc-ee's gas station.

We had no real reason to go there other than "go to this while in Texas." It basically is a fancy gas station with well marketed merchandise, which led me to get a t-shirt. We arrived at the Texas Motor Speedway at around 1 pm and my goodness was it hot. I thought Texas heat was always exaggerated, but once we walked around a bit, I soon figured out it wasn't. I started to see all my drifting icons that I had watched online in the pits with their crew with their cars, Ryan Tuerck's Ferrari FRS, Forrest Wang's S14, Vaughn Gittin Jr.'s Mustang, and many more legends in FD. An energy drink company was giving out free drinks to anyone that asked for them. Truman and I went up to a few different people handing out these drinks and pretty soon we had consumed several of these energy drinks over the course of a few hours. The heat must've gotten to me at one point because while I took a break at this table outside the concession stand, I had fallen asleep. I woke up about an hour later to Charlie tapping me on the shoulder, asking if I was okay. After I realized I just took a nap at a racetrack, I got up feeling refreshed and ready for the rest of the day. We sat up in the stands later that evening and watched as each of the drivers battled on the track. I wasn't taking that bad of pictures as I expected without the lens I had forgotten. My automatic 20-70mm lens did just fine tracking the cars as they went around the track. I'd been to a few "grassroots" drift events, but this was drifting to the highest level. Entering corners sideways at well over 100mph and maintaining a perfected route each time through the track. It was truly incredible seeing the raw talent that many of those drivers possessed. The top 4 of the event wrapped up the night with Chelsea Denofa, Fredric Asbo, James Deane, and Piotr Więcek, competing for the podium positions. Asbo got 3rd place over Denofa with a crazy chase run, then it came down to the two teammates James Deane and Piotr Więceck for the finals. The battle between these two were extremely intense, the crowd was going insane over how close these two runs were. Both of their chase and lead runs were amazing and that made it difficult to judge. My camera died just before their last battle so I never was able to capture the moment of who won. Piotr Więcek came out with the win just barely ahead of Deane, he celebrated with a few victory donuts while the entire crowd was cheering. I was thoroughly exhausted after that day and ready to take another nap. Just before midnight, we stopped by an In-N-Out Burger that was across the street from the racetrack. In-N-Out is an exclusive restaurant to a few states, Texas included. It was my first time having In-N-Out and I held high expectations from the craze I heard about this fast food place. Part of what In-N-Out Burger is known for is their old school paper hats that they give to customers, of course I had to get one along with my meal. Truth be told, I believe In-N-Out burger did live up to the hype. The burger was incredible along with the fries and chocolate milkshake. With a full and happy belly, it was time to hit the hotel for the night. We arrived with all of our free Formula Drift stuff and wearing our hats from In-N-Out. The room was nice, we had a TV, and there was a 24/7 hot tub out in the back. Later that night, we all went out to the hot tub to relax after our long day. Who knew a sunburn would feel great in a 90 degree pool. Before we knew it, it was 1 in the morning and here we were, chilling in a hot tub in the middle of Texas.

October was a great month, everyday some of us would come home from school and chill out at Truman's house. Nothing was better than lazily sitting on that couch talking to your best friends after school every day. Every so often we would get spontaneous ideas to go do something fun, such as visiting the lake, downtown, and occasionally goofing around in grocery stores. We goofed around in Target and Walmart a bunch, going down the aisles and laughing at anything we could make a joke out of. Toilet paper forts were a great way of spending our time in Target. Haines' brother Scott and I would shape loads of the toilet paper bundles to make hallways and chairs all throughout the aisle. Since it was getting closer to Halloween, we got creative on what funny stuff we could do in a store. We were sitting around at Truman's house when someone got the idea that it would be funny to dress up as the Grim Reaper and casually go grocery shopping. Truman had a Grim Reaper costume so we spent a few minutes perfecting his look before heading to the store. We arrived in Target with our group and Truman dressed as the Grim Reaper. We had Truman go over to the oranges and carefully inspect them to play it off like he was actually searching for groceries. Needless to say we were getting many concerned looks from the workers and customers, but it was one of the funniest things we had done yet. We were walking down one of the aisles and a girl screamed out across the store "I've been waiting for so long!" We all immediately busted out laughing. Within the next ten minutes, a group of Target workers and security guards came over to us and said we needed to leave because it was scaring some of the customers. I highly doubted that was true, but it was fun while it lasted.

During our senior year we had two dances, Homecoming and Prom. Since I had a ton of fun at Homecoming the previous year, I was excited about this next one. Like I wore my diamond grill and chains last year, Colby had fake Yeezy shoes that lit up on the bottom. He had been talking about them for weeks and they arrived at his house the day before the dance. Our whole group met up at a park to take pictures for our families, we did some funny poses and even lifted Colby up across our arms in one of the pictures. It was always better to dances much later than it started, therefore we purposely waited 30 minutes to an hour before getting there. Our homecoming was in the lunchroom and felt weird dressing formally and dancing to loud music in that place. Once our group met up and Colby turned on his shoes, it was game on. I feel like we grew confidence after our first couple of dances. Since we were older and upperclassmen, it gave us more courage to do crazier stuff and be more outgoing. We put Rogers on top of Brody's shoulders as they danced around, we all were screaming and going wild while Rogers was throwing his hands in the air like he was on top of the world. We had the majority of the room looking at us cheering, it was so awesome with all of us having such a good time. After the dance we all went back to Brayden's house out in the country. It's always a surreal feeling heading home after a school dance, like it's the end of a movie where the main character has had the best night of their life. Most of us slept on the floor while trying to avoid Brayden's younger brother from shooting us with Nerf guns with thumb tacks in the darts, there truly was never a dull moment that night.

By this time, I was finally finished with painting my wheels. After all the struggles of getting the paint to adhere properly, it finally worked. I got the wheels put on and I was rocking some new gloss black wheels for the rest of the year. I told myself I'd either never attempt to spray paint again or get an air compressed spray gun. It shouldn't have taken that long to paint a set of wheels, but experience is a hard teacher.

In school, weight training was becoming a lot of fun. After our regular workouts at the beginning of class, our teacher, who was one of the football coaches, would let us do our own workouts for the remainder of class. Doing our own workouts turned into goofing around and socializing most of the time. Brayden was also in that class and we got to become good friends with a lot of people there. I miss that class a lot because it was hilarious and there were a lot of great people, including our teacher who we called "coach." Coach would tell us all sorts of life stories, like the time he had hip replacement surgery, an ATV accident at his grandparents' house, and many stories from college. We did a multitude of stupid things in that class that it's hard to recount. People would change into their gym clothes before and after class in this room in the back of the gym. This room was all sorts of torn up from the previous goofballs who were in there, rips in the carpet, broken lockers, parts of the ceiling were missing, it looked rough. This is where most of the shenanigans occurred during this class. One time a couple of our friends tried stacking each other on top of Brayden's shoulders, they almost we're able to reach the ceiling until one person lost their balance and all three of them came crashing down on one another. There even was a time where some kids would climb up this ladder into the ceiling. I'm not sure why there was a fixed ladder on the wall, but there was and kids took advantage of it. There was one kid who climbed up into the ceiling and Coach walked in the room shortly after asking where the kid was. All of us were holding back laughing as we said he was in the bathroom. Some kids would pretend to fight, have arm wrestling competitions, all sorts of stuff besides actually working out.

Jon's birthday that year was one to remember, we started off the night by playing Cards Against Humanity, then we played musical chairs in Jon's living room. At some point during the night, we stuck the rim of solo cups in our mouth. It had no purpose other than looking funny, we eventually got a group picture with all of us with solo cups in our mouth. It was ridiculous but it was equally as funny. The next day our school was supposed to tour a college campus that took up our whole day for school. It was an option whether we wanted to visit the campus or not, I knew that I could go visit this campus on my own time if I wanted to so I'd much rather spend that time doing something else. I spontaneously had the idea to make a bunch of sandwiches and skate around downtown to give to the homeless. I wanted to have the feeling of doing something nice for someone and this was a great way, it also would spread the message that skaters are friendly. I pitched the idea to Zach, who also did not go on the tour, and he said he would gladly join me. I went ahead and bought all the stuff needed to put together about 12 ham and bologna sandwiches. I met up at Zach's house where we sat down and made the sandwiches on the kitchen counter. We put them in our backpack and headed off downtown. It was early in the morning and we had a load of sandwiches to hand out. We skated around downtown because a lot of homeless people tend to live and walk around there. Riding down street after street, we would come across people who looked down on their luck and in rough shape. We simply would approach them and ask them if they wanted a sandwich for free, we had ones with ketchup, mayo, or plain. Most of the people were appreciative of the food, though there were a couple that seemed a little ungrateful by not saying thank you or having an attitude like they were entitled to have it, either way I felt like I was doing the right thing. After we had finished giving away the last sandwich, we skated a little bit on the obstacles downtown before heading back home. A couple hours later, we hung out at Colby's house. This is when we started to hang out at Colby's house a bit more during the year, his room had a comfortable feel to it with his ambient LED lights and cozy seats. He had recently got a virtual reality system and it was comical to watch all of us attempt to play the different games. After hanging at Colby's for a bit, we decided to go downtown. By this point, we had explored just about everything and were running out of new ideas to do. Rentable electric scooters recently came to our town and were growing in popularity, this gave us a new idea. Truman, Monaghan, Colby, Haines, his brother Scott and I all rented scooters to ride around downtown. There rarely was any traffic downtown at night and that allowed us to ride the scooters all in the street. I tried all sorts of tricks on the scooter like jumping off the curb, sitting while riding, and drifting with one foot down. We rode up to the parking garage downtown, where we hung out on top, gazing at the lights from the surrounding buildings. Those scooters were awesome and it was definitely not the last time we would do that. The next day I hung out at Haines' house, Jack was telling me how he and his brother were trying to fix up their parents' old golf cart. Original steering wheel, no roof, and a wooden cargo bay. Once they got it running, we drove it all around the neighborhood, on the road, through trails, and even Jack's brother and I went through a fast food drive through on it. That was one of the funniest moments I remember with that golf cart. We set up cones in the nearby parking lot outside of his neighborhood and acted like it was a race course. We all had a blast taking turns riding it and pushing its limits on the trails.

Computer programming in school was eating me alive and there was no way I would make it the rest of the year without failing. Most of that first semester wasn't bad and I found myself often completing my work early, it was only towards the end did it start to get difficult. I told myself all I had to do was make it the rest of the semester and I would switch classes. The only problem was that in order to graduate I needed to have two years of computer classes and I only had one semester in total. For some reason, my three years of computer repair class didn't count, that's why I took programming. I took the chance of not taking another computer class and see if they actually would hold me accountable by the time I graduated. By the end of that semester in programming, the whole class had let loose. I was friends with a number of people in that class and after we would complete our work, we would all join a mutual game server on Counter Strike. What was ironic was that the majority of internet games were blocked on school computers, but we found a website that allowed us to play Counter Strike online. Our teacher often got irritated once she saw the majority of the class playing Counter Strike instead of doing their work. I had some of the most amusing times from school in that class, looking forward to leveling up weapons, beating the levels, and competing with everyone in the class. It reminded me of the glory days of beating Run 2 in a single semester during Freshman year. The balance between school work and video games was a true key to my academic success. Pep rallies for football games also were starting to become more fun. Our entire school met in the gym stadium and played music, games, and the teachers never failed to come up with more embarrassing choreography. I enjoyed it though, because I got to hang out with my friends and it was an excuse to leave class for an hour.

Having a passion for cars and anything with an engine. I had the urge to tinker with something with a small engine. Haines had a few projects that we helped him work on and that inspired me to do the same. I was fascinated with the idea of buying a run-down toy, fixing it up, and selling it for profit. On one cold night in December Jack and I set out to pick up a mini bike that I had my eye on. Little did I know this was another hard series of lessons I would learn. It was an old Chinese pocket bike with a 50cc motor, plastic body pieces, and an aluminum frame. I knew that the original motor did not run and I planned on swapping it for a 212cc engine. For the next three months, this was my new toy to fix up and play with. A couple days later Truman, Charlie, and I were driving around in a town that we rarely visited. We came across an ice rink that was set up where you could rent ice skates and skate around. For it being December, it was close to 60 degrees outside and I was wearing jeans and a t-shirt. We went over to the ice rink and got our skates. It was only us on the ice rink while we were there and it was hilarious watching the guys learn how to maneuver on the ice. It felt like we were in a Hallmark movie on a low budget as I attempted to spin while jumping, ultimately falling multiple times. I went home later that night to continue working on the pocket bike. I had bought a new motor and had the bike torn down to the frame. I came to the realization that the motor was too big to fit on the original mounting place. This posed a huge problem and meant that I would need custom fabrication in order for it to fit. I had to grit my teeth and accept this was out of my skill range to do alone. I had to work on other tasks such as motor modifications, new throttle assembly, and painting the body pieces, until I got around to taking it to a fabrication shop. For the paint design, I decided to have a "sharpie bike" style where the entire bike was designed from hand drawn sharpie designs. I had seen this done a few times on other bikes and I wanted to try it out. For hours I would sit in my room trying to come up with random designs to draw on the plastic body pieces. It took quite a long time, but it turned out looking way better than I imagined. This year's winter break was filled with great laughs and new adventures, but I knew my final semester of high school was creeping up whether I liked it or not.

14

The Last Ride

2018 was coming to an end with 2019 on the horizon. It was weird to think that I was graduating that year, as if one day it was only my first day of high school, then I looked up and it was five months until it was my last. I always thought it was funny when people would publicly state their new year's resolution, to then never commit to them. The phrase "new year, new me!" was getting outplayed, as almost every person who said that thought it would change them from doing drugs and finding fake love in a Whataburger parking lot. The only new year's resolution I had at the time was finishing the mini bike, getting a new camera, and getting a new job, and I was determined to fulfill all three. On New Year's Eve, a couple of us went mudding in Haines' Jeep outside of the Titan complex. It had rained the day before, therefore the dirt was in prime condition for the Jeep to handle. After we got Jack's Jeep looking like a slice of chocolate cake, we headed to Jon's house to have our New Year's party. Jon had recently bought a set of boxing gloves for us to mess around with anytime we were hanging out. Two people at a time went into the backyard and competed in multiple rounds of boxing, while the rest of everyone watched above on the deck. While watching Brayden and Colby fight, I remember thinking someone was going into the new year with less teeth. We all sat in the living room, watching the ball in Time Square slowly sink to the bottom, then all of sudden it was 2019. All of us were blowing party horns and going crazy that we had successfully made it around the sun one more year. To celebrate, we had to raise a toast. Being underage, sparkling grape juice was the next-best-thing. We went out to the back porch where we struggled to get the bottle open. Then Haines got the idea to use his belt buckle as a bottle opener. He grabbed the bottle, undid his belt, and snapped the cap right off the bottle with the drink spraying everywhere, that's how we started the new year.

January was a wild month as well. I was looking for a Job at the time and Brayden worked at a dealership. He told me they were hiring for a lot porter position and that sounded like something I would enjoy doing. I went down there, talked to the managers down at the dealership, interviewed, and got the Job in the same day. I could tell I was going to enjoy this job because my managers and the person who trained me were really unique people. Later that night, me and some of the guys went to the memorial races. It was kind of rainy outside so there weren't as many cars as there usually were. I was standing behind Truman who was trying to help someone pull back on something super hard. Once his arm shot back after it was released from pulling, his elbow accidentally hit me in the nose. The impact was so sudden, I didn't know what had happened at first. Truman immediately apologized, but we both knew it was a complete accident. I first thought my teeth were knocked out because I got hit just below the nose, but after we inspected my face, I looked to be alright. My nose and teeth were hurting for the next couple hours or so. After Memorial, we headed back to Haines' house to hang out. At his house my nose still didn't feel right, I got a hold of it and felt if anything was broken. I got a shocking feeling as I felt a separated bone beneath my nose move freely. I didn't know what else to do besides leave it alone and hope it grew back normally. I didn't have my car with me at Jack's house, therefore I either needed someone to drop me off at my house or have my mom pick me up. Though there was another idea I came up with, running home. I've always liked running, especially spontaneous ventures that involve running. Jack lived about four miles from my house and it had started raining, adding a bit of spice to the journey. I told Jack that I wanted to attempt to run home in the rain, everyone looked at me like I had four eyes. I told them in the event that if I got too exhausted, I'd call for a ride, but I wanted to see if I could do this. I set out running from his house at a steady pace leaving the neighborhood and enroute to my house. About a mile down the road, Truman and Jon passed me as they were heading home. We both waved and I could see them laughing as I agreed this was quite silly that I committed to doing this. Eventually I made it back to my house, fatigued and soaking wet. I didn't tell my parents that I had run home from Jack's house, as they were confused as to why I was drenched and muddy. I then went on to explain why that was the cherry on top of my day. I got a job, broke my nose, and ran four miles in the rain, all in the same day.

I had another electric scooter adventure downtown a few weeks later. I was with Jon, Charlie, Colby, and Haines as it was 30 degrees that night, but we were determined to tear up the streets on the scooters. We rode up and down the roads as I could barely feel my hands from them freezing. We drove up to the parking garage that we would climb on the roof of. There was an elevator in the middle so we didn't have to walk all the way up and we got the idea of taking our scooters with us inside the elevator. It was a tight ride, being five guys and five electric scooters crammed in this single elevator. Once we were at the top, we drove around a bit before climbing the ladder to the top of the roof. We weren't there too long as it was getting colder and colder as the night went on. The more time we spent standing around the base of the ladder, we thought a heater was more of a priority than food or water. As we all were bundled up, trying to hold on to the little warmth we had left, the weather got the best of us and we headed home early.

After finishing the body pieces, getting the engine in, and numerous random issues, the mini bike was finished. I brought it out in the driveway to do a test drive. It started right up and I took it around the block to make sure everything was running right. I had done it, after so much hard work and probably more money than I wanted to spend, it was done. I was thrilled to hear it start up and hold a steady idle. This not only meant I was done working on it, but I could finally sell it. A month later, a kid about my age picked up the bike and I had just barely completed my goal of making a profit from it. Working at the dealership was going awesome after my first month. My favorite part about it was that since I was over at the used cars lot, I got to drive all sorts of different cars. Within the first two weeks, I got to drive a manual supercharged Subaru BRZ. The month after that, I got to drive a modified 2011 Ford Mustang Shelby GT500 that made around 700 horsepower. Right before I headed to the gas station to fill it up, my manager came over to me in the window and said "be careful, this thing is really fast." He was not wrong when he said that, the car would taunt me not to floor it as the supercharger wined up when I barely pressed the gas. It was loud, mean, and I knew whoever owned it would definitely have their fun with it. I also got to drive everything between lifted Jeeps, Trucks, and SUVs. Brayden and I also had a bunch of fun getting to hang out occasionally and picking up food for the dealership. The stories weren't as top tier as the cash wash yet, but I was still having a blast.

Along with school, work, and finishing the bike, I wanted to learn how to backflip. I had almost mastered front flipping off of anything, but I felt like learning a backflip was the next step up. I spent months researching how to do them and practicing for many days on my trampoline. The key trick that helped me learn them was practicing a cartwheel, but turning more and more to the side, to where eventually it's a back handspring. Doing back handsprings got me in the motion of doing a backflip. Most all videos say to do a backflip, I just have to commit to the motion. The scariest part of doing something new is committing. My sister was on the trampoline with me and I told her to film as I would give my full effort to attempt a backflip. On February 9th, 2019, I did my first backflip ever. I threw my hands up, jumped, tuck, rolled, and landed. It was a weird feeling, but I had done it. I was screaming in excitement, it reminded me of learning a hard skateboarding trick, when I thought It's be impossible to learn but eventually I landed it. Once I did the motion for the first time, it's almost impossible not to do it again. It was a piece of cake after that first one and I kept doing backflips one after another. One of the reasons why I pursued learning them was so I could do them at the lake off small jumps and other obstacles.

As I became more acclimated with the new school semester, my routines changed a bit. I no longer sat in my car every day. After I would get my lunch, I would ride with Brayden and Colby to the gas station to get their food, then we would hang out in the school parking lot until class started. In my history through film class I was friends with a few people in there who were no short of class clowns. Though it worked out because the teacher was also a sarcastic guy and had lots of fun messing with us on assignments and class discussions. I sat at a table with no one I knew, but what I did know was that the girl sitting diagonal from me was something out of a dream. Most of the attractive girls at my school were copy and pasted from each other, their looks and personality were all the same. Every so often, I would notice one that was unique of their own, this girl in my history through film class was one of them. Gorgeous brown hair, sweet smile, and eyes that absolutely melted me, her name was Katie. I knew she was more on the popular side, but I felt like I had a chance if I got to know her; that was my new mission to achieve by the end of the year.

I finally got around to getting myself a new camera. All my tips from the car wash helped me fund it, a Canon 5D MkII, full frame and 21 megapixels of sweet photography goodness. This was the next step in my photography journey and the car page would soon get a whole lot better. Later that month, I went with Haines to trade his newly restored dirt bike for two more dirt bikes. We met up with the guy about an hour away and on our way there we saw the cutest dog at a gas station. In the backseat of this car was this giant, polar bear-like dog with the cutest face. We couldn't help but stop and look at this giant ball of fluff in the backseat of this car. Once we met up with the guy and traded the dirt bikes, we drove to a place to drive them around for a bit. We happened to drive to the Stroud drift lot, which was the same place I had ridden in my first drift car at a drift event. We unstrapped the two dirt bikes and rode them all around the giant concrete lot. We had so much fun ripping around those small dirt bikes in that huge space until eventually heading back home. A couple days later, I went to a skateboarding competition, six years after my first one. Everyone got free pizza and drinks during the contest. I had gotten much better since my first contest, but I didn't expect to beat my competitors. I signed up in the second highest division and prayed I would do good. It was cloudy and chilly, therefore I had to skate around for a while to make sure my muscles were warm. It's almost impossible to skate decently when cold. Once it was competition time, I gave it my all. I had skated at this park a bunch and I had a great line planned out for my run. There was one kid in my division who did a 360 flip to 50-50 grind and there was no chance I was getting first place after that. I ended in third place and I was honestly quite satisfied with that, given my competition. I got some free stickers, more pizza, and by the end of the contest my legs were fried. I hammocked with the guys later that night and we thought it'd be a lot warmer than it was but we found ourselves bundled up in our hammocks as it was 35 degrees and drizzling rain.

The next day we were hanging out at Colby's house that night. He invited some friends over from our school that I kind of knew, but not well. One of their friends was from a different School, this was Sam. All throughout the night Colby and his other friends were telling me that Sam thought I was cute. I didn't think much of it as I don't take information like that too seriously. As the night went on, all these friends were urging me to go over and talk to her, so I did. I didn't have many words to say because I did not know this girl at all and was nervous because I felt like I was being forced to talk to this girl, though I didn't mind because she turned out to be cool. I got up from the futon and went back over to talk with Colby, Truman, Jon, and the others. They all were whispering that I should go over and make a move, I looked at them like they had just told me to run my car off a bridge. I was not going to make a move on this girl in front of seven other people in Colby's room, maybe I would if it was a different situation but I came to the conclusion that this was not the time or place. It was awkward for me the rest of the night because I had this all in the back of my head, but I tried to brush it off. We all continued to hangout, listen to music, and play the virtual reality game the rest of the night before heading home.

Before I knew it was getting close to my last spring break of high school. March was a crazy month all together, but we had a list of stuff planned out like bonfires, Memorial, and our second trip to Arkansas. A couple days prior, Haines and I did some exploring down by the beach spot on a day that we didn't have school. We brought down a BB gun and a machete to play with as we explored all in the woods and on the beach. It was around midday and I remember enjoying the amazing weather while riding on the roof rack of Jack's Jeep on the trails. We found empty beer cans at one of the bonfire spots to set up in the sand and shoot with the BB gun. There was something special about hanging down at the beach spot during the day. I could see everything and it felt like I was seeing the beach spot in a better light, literally. Later that night, our whole group and a few more of our friends came to the beach spot for a bonfire. We brought down a ton of pallets, gasoline, and spare wood. While we were hanging out, one of us noticed there was a pile of glass bottles in one area near the fire. We got some of the bottles, filled them with gasoline and threw them into the fire to see if it would blow up like a Molotov cocktail. It kind of did what we were expecting but it wasn't too big of a fire. We then found an empty handle of liquor to fill with gas, this was about three times the amount of gasoline that we had previously tried. I looked at the bottle thinking there was no way this wasn't going to be huge. We all got in a position far away from the fire, then our friend got the bottle, did a couple swings, and chunked it into the fire. We heard the bottle shatter as a giant fireball, that was about 20 feet tall, ignited into the sky. It was a wonderful sight to witness that much gasoline being set ablaze. We also threw pieces of Styrofoam, that had washed up on the beach, into the fire and watched how that melted apart in the fire. Similar to the composition of tires in a way, slowly melting with the contents dripping away with a blue and orange tint.

The next day was the first official day of spring break. A couple of us went to a car meet that morning, then I went with Haines to wash his Jeep from the night before. We did a lot of hammocking during this break because the weather was starting to get warm and it definitely felt better than being cold in the rain. We dedicated that second day to go on our annual Arkansas trip. Before we went to the waterfall and restaurant, we discovered this place on the edge of Arkansas where people can take a tour of this giant underground cave. We got there before the cave even opened, which allowed us to spend time looking around the valley of greenery that this cave tour was by. When it was time for us to go on the tour it was only our group and maybe two other people. The cave was amazing, it's similar to the Marvel Cave in Silver Dollar City, but a bit smaller. This cave once housed a group of Spanish conquistadors in the 1800s who were traveling through from Mexico. Being in Indian territory, the Native Americans spotted their campfire smoke from a natural chimney out of the top of the cave. The Natives then went inside and killed all the Spaniards, except one. The one Spaniard buried all the gold, treasure, and other valuables deep in the cave so the natives could not find it. The cave owner told us the treasure has yet to be discovered, but they brought out a shaman who said the treasure is present in the cave. The tour was awesome, seeing the caverns and all the rock formations that were woven all throughout the inside of this cave. Following the cave tour, we went to our beloved restaurant in

Fayetteville, JJ's. We played cards against humanity again while waiting for our food. Charlie got a call while we were sitting there and it was his manager from work, Charlie had forgotten to call off work that day. He quickly got up from the table and went outside while on the phone. He was pacing back and forth outside the restaurant as all of us could barely sit still as we laughed so hard at how funny this was. He came back inside and said he was supposed to go into work in five minutes, but here he was in another state. That was one of the funniest moments from that whole trip. The food was great as always and before we knew it, we were on to the waterfall. We walked around and explored a bit more of the trails. We made sure to explore more of the park and see all the scenic views that surrounded the waterfall before hammocking at the bottom. The weather was remarkably nice and the water coming off of the mountain looked as clear as tap water. We hammocked for a while as we listened to music, enjoying the peaceful atmosphere as we laid back and relaxed. On the last few days of spring break, I sold the mini bike and two days later Haines bought a couple of baby ducks. We all went over and played with them as they were able to fit snugly in your hand, one was yellow and the other was brown. The funniest part about these ducks is that one of them was going to be named Ketamine, which is a drug used as horse tranquilizer. We thought that would be too harsh to be constantly calling this duck Ketamine, therefore we came up with the more innocent name of Joey and Chandler, from the characters of the show "Friends," then we made their last name Ketamine. Jack had now become the proud father of two beautiful ducks named Joey and Chandler Ketamine.

Two days later, my sister and I went to a Travis Scott concert. It was actually our second attempt at going because the last one got cancelled because of production issues. The show was awesome, Travis put on a great concert with all my favorite songs from him. He rode a roller coaster on the ceiling which made it more believable why they had issues last time. There were fireworks, lazers, and explosions that synced with the beat of the songs. The next day looked like our school was going on a Travis Scott field trip because the majority of kids wore Travis Scott t-shirts that were from the concert last night. I also realized that Prom was four days away and I still did not have a date. Our group were hanging out at Haines' house when we were discussing what to do about my Prom situation. It was almost an obligation to find me a date so I could say I had one for my Senior Prom. All the guys were questioning me on who at our school would I be willing to take to Prom. I gave them a look like I was just asked to figure out the circumference of the sun, I had no idea. I thought about Katie, but I didn't know her well enough to take her to Prom. I couldn't come up with anyone that was a solid candidate to go to Prom with. Then they proposed that I take our good friend Julie, the same person who I made friends with on the bus during middle school with Jon. For some reason I was hesitant on the idea of that, maybe I was subconsciously wanting to take Katie, but faced with a weird situation. Jack, Scott, Jon, Truman, Brayden, all were fed up with my indecisiveness and jokingly grabbed me, tied me up, and sat on me on the floor, begging me to take Julie to the Prom. With all my limbs immobile, my friend's dog-piling on me, and less than 96 hours away from Prom, I figured I was out of options. I agreed to take Julie and they all got off and untied me, it certainly was some needed tough love. Now with my date selected, we ran into the issue of getting the Prom ticket for Julie. I had one but they had stopped selling them at school a few days prior. Then we had a lightbulb moment of somehow duplicating my Prom ticket. Haines' dad said it would be possible to scan and copy a replica ticket. He said this was a trick he used during college to duplicate homework sheets. The trick was that we had to get this perfect in order to work. It was slimmer than an index card, multiple colors, and our principal's signature on the back that we had to line up perfectly. The night before prom, we went back over to Jack's house, his dad got out his colored printer, and we laid my original ticket on the scanner. On the first couple of tries, the design was a little skewed and not aligned. After several tries, it all lined up and the colors weren't bad. We held the original ticket up to the one we had just printed and it was like they were identical twins. We screamed in celebration that we had just successfully replicated my Prom ticket. We cut it out of the printer paper we copied it on so I could take it to my mom to finalize. Our whole group drove from

Haines' to mine in an escorting fashion like my newly copied Prom ticket was the President. We all got on a Bluetooth call like it was a Walkie-talkie shouting

"The ticket is secured!"

"Bravo leader checking in!"

"Escorting the package now!"

We then brought it home to my mom where she matched the colors with a colored pencil. Though the ticket was only good if it actually worked and that was the next test. We carried out Prom day as normal by everyone in our group meeting at this park outside of downtown. We took a bunch of pictures with our dates, family, and our whole group. We then went to dinner at a fancy restaurant to kick off the formal spirit of the night. Our waitress paid compliments to Colby's hair, as he was known for having long, wavy, black hair that he had been growing out for years. Colby even allowed her to braid his hair as we all were amazed that our waitress was this friendly to be doing that. After eating, we arrived at prom and it happened to be the same venue that we were invited to by the girls who we hung out with during Sophomore year. Truman, Jon, and I joked that in a way we were ending high school in the same place it started. We went up to the front where we would be checked by security and show them our tickets. I handed Julie the copied ticket and hoped for the best. Without a second glance, she got in just fine and the ticket worked. Once we all got inside we were jumping around in celebration that we all got in and the ticket worked, now we were ready to get the night started. The music surprisingly wasn't that bad and we were satisfied with how they set up the venue. We were all excited and ready to go wild. We got the idea to toss our friend Emilie up in the air. Brayden, Zach, Charlie, and a few others got underneath her and tossed her like a cheerleader in the air. This was hilarious as we had the whole venue looking at us because we were tossing this girl six feet in the air several times. I'm surprised the teachers didn't say anything because this was totally unsafe, but it was in the moment. We carried on the tradition of throwing Rogers up on someone's shoulders and we got Colby on top of Brody's shoulders at the same time. We were all going crazy by screaming and jumping and high as we could go. I've never gone that crazy at a school dance, but by the end of the night, I was trying to wear out the fabric in my suit. One of the funniest moments from that night was that Jon hopped in a Conga line that was starting. I thought I should go ahead and hop in as well, so I got right behind him. The line grew all throughout the crowd and we had everyone singing and dancing like something out of a movie. I have never had more fun at a school dance than this one, and I thought I went wild the year before. We heard that one of our friends was having a Prom after party and that's where we decided to go when we left. When I got there, most everyone was several cups deep in "apple juice" and the music from the speakers were shaking the house. Our group had a great time hanging out in the pool table room, where

Brayden and Colby dominated everyone the entire night. The next day we went hammocking at a park, reminiscing on all the best moments from the night before.

When we returned back to school, all I could think about was that the next big event was graduation. I was trying to make every day count up until that day. Brayden, Colby, and I went to the arcade every day during lunch. We all had online classes that added another hour of free time on top of our lunch time. We would blast classic rock songs from ACDC, Ozzy Osbourne, and Mötley Crüe all the way down the road to the arcade. We spent that time at the arcade only playing pool. Brayden and Colby were pros compared to me, which made me try extra hard if I wanted to get close to their level. Eventually I got better towards the end of the year, but so did they. After we spent a couple of months wearing out the pool table at the arcade, we started going to Colby's house during our virtual hour. There we spent playing with the virtual reality system and hanging out listening to music. Sometimes Brayden and I would wrestle on the floor to get the other person to tap out. Brayden loved wrestling people and it was great practice for me since I had little experience. Brayden was no doubt the stronger person but there were times I had a chance at victory.

On a rainy day in April, a few of us were hanging out at Truman's house and we were brainstorming ideas on what to do that day. I suggested that we go pool hopping, which is where we go to a random neighborhood and jump in people's pools, one after another. I had heard many pool hopping stories before and I was itching to do this so badly because this sounded insanely fun. I got them on the idea of doing this and we passed it onto the rest of the group to see who all would come. Most of the group was on board and we sat down and discussed how it was going to work. We pulled up the map of our city and went to a neighborhood that wasn't too far from us. We found a string of eight houses with pools, and that was perfect. To add to this, it was pouring rain, but it didn't matter because we were going to get wet anyway. We quickly went home, changed into swimsuits, and met up in a parking lot. We then went over the game plan, Truman would park at the end of the street where we would come out, we would walk to the start of the houses, jump through all the pools along the strip, and meet Truman at the end. Truman pulled up to the curb, where we would later meet him, with the dry towels ready. Six of us hopped out of the car in the pouring rain, walking down the street with nothing but our swim trunks. We were chuckling on our way to the start because anyone who saw us would be a bit confused. We made it to the first house on the start of the street, we all looked at the first wooden fence that was in front of us, gave a countdown, and the pool hopping began. I almost had trouble hopping the first fence due to my laughing because I couldn't believe we were actually doing this. We crash landed in the first pool, sending huge splashes everywhere.

Adrenaline was at peak flow as I hopped out of the water in the first backyard. The next fence was a piece of cake, as I hopped over with ease and dove into the next pool with everyone. After the fourth or fifth pool, we came across a backyard with a couple of dogs that sounded like they weren't too pleased to see us. As we were standing on the fence, contemplating if we wanted to risk getting our keisters bit off, we made the decision to take a shortcut out of the yard we were in and hightail it to the car. As we were climbing over the fence back out to the street, this family across the street were going out to their car at the same time. They gave us a blank stare as they saw six guys in swimsuits in the pouring rain, hop over this person's fence and start sprinting down the street. It was a race to Truman's car as all of us struggled to get traction in the wet grass. I ran as fast as possible, trying not to pay attention to the family who was most likely on the phone with local authorities soon. We made it into the car, diving through the doors one after another. Laughing hysterically as we got our towels and made it out from the neighborhood unscathed.

As we only had a couple dozen bonfires that year, the one after we went pool hopping was one for the record books. We planned on having a bonfire one night, but we also saw many other kids heading down to the river as well. We invited a lot of people because we were looking forward to this fire. We met up with all the people in a parking lot by a soccer field, where we had a convoy to come down with to the beach spot. Haines brought everyone blue Kool-Aid drinks and we piled into his Jeep. On our way through the trails to the bonfire, we were leading the pack of trucks and Jeeps. Colby and our friend Aaron, were riding on top of the Jeep as I was hanging out of the window while we were blasting "Kickstart My Heart" by Mötley Crüe. I was ready to have a great time with my friends and see what the night brought. When we got to the spot, a small fire was already going and there were about thirty people. As the night went on, more and more people started showing up and there were trucks and Jeeps all over the beach spot with people riding in the back. The fire had gotten bigger and towards the end of the night, there had to be around two hundred people. We all were standing around Jack's Jeep when we couldn't believe how many people there were and thought this might've been one of the biggest bonfires we've had. We got word that there were cops driving around the roads near the beach spot entrances. It was always a flip-of-a-coin if it was worth leaving a bonfire in order not to be blocked in by police. Since the fire was starting to die out, we made the choice to pack up and get out of there early. Sure enough, about fifteen minutes later, we saw the cops swarm the beach spot and start pulling everyone over who was trying to escape. That was always an aspect of the river I never understood. There was a huge sign that permitted people to shoot fireworks, loiter, and ride ATVs there because it was technically a recreational off-road park, but when people had bonfires, the city got upset. There were a couple times when I had to run through the woods during a bonfire because the cops came down and ambushed everyone, but 90% of the time we didn't have that problem.

Haines picked up a cheap welder for him to practice on and a few of us got the chance to try it out as well. It was an old electric stick welder that put out a small amount of amps, but still welded most objects just fine. We played around with this welder a ton at Jack and Truman's house, piecing together random parts of metal and learning the proper ways to form arcs. One time at Truman's house, we welded together a spoiler and attached it on the back of a scooter, burning the initials "TTP" on the top of it. One funny part I remember from this time was when we were practicing on a cooking pan and ants would crawl all over it. We thought it'd be funny to see what would happen if we tired welding on the ants. All it took was one zap of the welder and the ant would instantaneously explode, it was borderline cruelty, but it was quite funny to watch. Around this time, Truman introduced us to Matt, who was one of his friends from tech school, who was also friends with the guy with the red Foxbody Mustang. Matt was super friendly and shared the common interest of cars. Matt began hanging out with us a bunch and getting to know more of the guys as the days went on, eventually becoming a part of our group. What's ironic, is that Matt sort of looks like me and we occasionally get mixed up if we're standing next to each other.

About a couple weeks into May, it was only a matter of time until the last day in this history through film class with this girl that I really liked. I didn't want to go on knowing that I didn't try asking this girl out before high school ended. I knew that I would deeply regret not doing something when I had a chance. As much as I was petrified to do this, I knew I had to. I talked a lot to Dawn, in my computer repair class, about how I should go about doing this. She told me to be confident and go for it. Very much easier said than done, but that's really all there was to it. I tried rehearsing what to say and making sure it sounded correct. There are many things in my life that I wish I had done differently, but this time I was going to say exactly what I wanted. We had just finished doing our end of the year project for the class where Katie, me, and one other person worked on a rap song to present. In that time, I got to talk to Katie and tried to get to know her. I felt like we had talked enough to where I could ask if she wanted to hang out. I didn't want to ask for her number, ask for her Snapchat, I wanted to see if she would accept getting to know someone face-to-face and that became the game plan. The tricky part was sometimes she wasn't in class or left early because it was towards the end of the year and our teacher didn't care if we showed up or not. I had to hope she would last until after class so I could ask her. The day came, where I knew by the end of class I would either ask her out or abort the mission. During the whole class I had a weird feeling of anxiousness and calmness, little did Katie know that I was borderline shaking in my seat thinking about it. As the minutes got closer to class getting out I thought, wow I'm really going to do this, I can't back out, I will do this. When the bell rang and class got out, I forced a wave of calmness and confidence through my body to prepare me for what was coming. I knew that Katie always walked to the right out of the classroom and I walked to the left, it took me everything I had to commit walking the other way to approach her.

"Hey Katie!" I said as she turned around and looked me directly in the eyes. I could not believe I was actually doing this. "Would you like to hangout sometime? I would really enjoy getting to know you better," as I said it confidently without a stutter.

"I would but I'm busy this week."

I was prepared for this, "I don't work next Tuesday if you want to then?"

She then gave me a look of uncertainty. "I'm not sure if that's going to work."

"Okay no problem, I just wanted to ask."

She walked off as I thought about if I said the right things. Should I have got her number just in case? Or was that a sign that she wasn't interested and wanted to be nice. I will never know, all I'm happy about is I at least tried. They say you miss 100% of the shots you don't take. I turned around and walked out the same door that I usually went out of, and headed to TSI. I walked in the door with a smile and Dawn looked up from her desk smiling also, as she knew what I had done. I told her what had happened and we laughed it off like it wasn't a big deal. I thought it worked out for me because if she said no, I wouldn't have to see her again. If she said yes, then my plan worked, it was a win-win. Life goes no matter what happens or doesn't happen and that's the beauty of going for it.

Our car shenanigans were far from over as we always seemed to be coming up with new ideas. Zach got a rental truck because one of his vehicles was getting worked on. Occasionally he would pick a few of us up and drive around in it. Even though it was a rental, we pushed this brand new truck to its limits. We were driving around town when we came across a railroad crossing with a steep hill on both sides. I was with Monaghan, Colby, and Zach when we all looked at each other like we were all thinking the same thing. We made sure our seatbelts were buckled and checked if NASA was watching because it was time to take-off! We got up speed to hit the jump just fast enough to get the front wheels off the ground. It was smooth as butter, so we went to try it again, this time going a bit faster than the last attempt. The impact was greater as every loose object in the truck levitated for a millisecond and the truck came crashing down, but still not all four wheels left the ground. We agreed to try one more time in an attempt to completely jump this truck. We got up more speed, reaching upwards of 45 mph. We were laughing and screaming as I could tell this would be the biggest jump. The front end flew up to where we couldn't even see the road, we floated up from our seats, and came crashing down like an atom bomb. Surprisingly, the truck was perfectly fine and we drove away as we were laughing uncontrollably. That wasn't our only adventure in the rental truck, donuts, burnouts, and off-roading were all action that the truck saw plenty of.

About a week before graduation, we decided we wanted to turn Zach's rental truck into a hot tub. We would lay a tarp down, fill it with water, and drive around town while swimming in the back. Everyone was beyond excited for this idea. It was later in the evening and most of the group gathered at Haines' house to prepare for this. We bought a big enough tarp to cover the truck bed and strapped it down with bungee cords. We had to make it in a way that it was impossible for water to leak through anywhere. Once the tarp was secured, it was time to add the water. We first got out the hose and held it up to the truck bed, the output amount of the water was not filling the truck fast enough. At the rate the hose was going at, it was going to be a while until it was done. We came up with the idea of filling the truck bed with pool water from the backyard, by transporting buckets back and forth. We first started out with a couple buckets that carried about a gallon or two of water, it was a little faster, but it could be more. What we came up with was an assembly line system of someone filling a bucket up from the pool, passing it on to someone at the fence gate, and running it out to the truck. This became peak efficiency for filling up the truck, soon the truck was minutes away from becoming full. We didn't want just a little bit of water, we wanted a full blown truck bed pool! The truck was now full and the fun was about to begin. Colby, Haines, Monaghan, Scott, Charlie, Brayden, and I all hop in the truck with Zach driving and Jon in the back filming us. The water neared the top of the truck bed, therefore Zach had to drive semi-carefully to spill as little water as possible. The carefulness lasted only a couple hundred feet as we got tossed all around the truck with giant waves crashing down anytime Zach floored or slammed on the brakes. This not only caused the loss of water, but huge waves being thrown in the road. Our first stop was the Whataburger drive through, a bunch of people from our school would meet up and hang out there. They got to witness seven guys in a truck bed pool pull up with water splashing everywhere. Everyone who saw us were laughing and smiling. We made our way to the drive through as we were lightly splashing water on the people behind us. It was beyond hilarious when we were relaxing in a pool, casually ordering fries and drinks. When we got up to the window, the workers looked at us in shock as we splashed water everywhere. We got our food and drove off, but not before sending a giant splash in the parking lot from Zach taking a hard turn. We drove around more in town and splashed water on people's cars at intersections if they smiled or gave us a thumbs up. It was priceless, I had the biggest smile on my face the entire time. After we had almost all the fun we wanted in this thing, we had to get the water out somehow. Of course we couldn't just open the tailgate, that would be too easy. A better way would be thrashing the truck around until all the water was thrown out. We went to an empty parking lot that was popular for kids to do donuts in and we were there for the same reason. As we got there, a couple kids in a truck pulled up and wanted to watch what we did. Zach sent the truck into a donut and sent water flying to one corner of the truck bed. All of us were screaming, holding on for dear life as the truck continued to spin in circles. Water was now leaving the truck bed at an astronomical rate. After we stopped and looked around, this parking lot had now turned into a waterpark. With most of the water gone and somehow all of us still in the truck bed, we headed back to Jack's house. With an empty truck bed and all of us exhausted, we unanimously agreed that this was one of the most entertaining things that we'd ever done. This was one of those events that I could see never getting tired of, it is that enjoyable.

Graduation was days away and we spent that time welding, hammocking, and playing at kid parks. I wanted to come up with some type of senior prank like toilet-papering the school or spraying silly string in the hallways, but our school was fairly uptight about that sort of stuff and I didn't want to get arrested for being funny. Before our actual graduation, we did a practice graduation that allowed us to go through the motions and give us an idea of how it was going to go. Our ceremony was at this college campus with a huge auditorium that could seat thousands of people. While our class met inside the building, about to practice walking out, all the lights went out. It was weird just standing in a dark room with little visibility, surrounded by your entire graduating class. The lights kept going off and that delayed us having to do the practice ceremony. It almost felt like a joke because of how uncoordinated this was. None of the teachers looked like they knew what they were doing and our instructions were being changed every five minutes. Then it came time for our actual graduation. Colby told us a few days prior that he was going to shave his head after graduation. I was excited for this because Colby had longer hair than any of us.

It was graduation day and we all walked in all dressed up and prepared to get a piece of paper saying we spent a certain amount of time in a chair required by the government. It was a weird night because during the ceremony, it started absolutely pouring. I sat there in my chair and couldn't help but listen to the monsoon of a rainstorm outside. It was crazy because the thunder would often crack off and it sounded like it was rough outside. Sure enough, about 20 minutes later the power goes out, keep in mind we're in this giant auditorium having our graduation ceremony and there's thousands of people, then all the lights in the entire place go out. The ceremony stops and everyone looks at each other like is this actually happening? We couldn't go on reading names because the microphone was dead, our principal got on stage with no microphone and he yelled to the audience, "it's okay, we will resume once we get the power back on." While that went on, we were stuck there twiddling our thumbs in the dark while they struggled to get the lights back on. It eventually turned back on and everyone started clapping like we had just landed on the moon. Having a last name that is towards the end of the alphabet, it took close to three hours until my name was called. I graduated with almost nine hundred other kids and they even had to read the names moderately fast so we weren't there all night. During the speeches from the valedictorians I couldn't help but think the speeches were cliche. Talking like robots with a fixed smile to the crowd, the lack of authenticity humored me. Though of course I had to give respect to those who spent too many hours studying just to get a colored rope that I could've ordered off of eBay. I get that some kids wanted to go that extra mile, but I'd much rather spend that time taking advantage of my teenage years. While I was accepting my diploma and taking my picture, I completely messed up shaking the guy's hand. How it was supposed to work was that I would walk up, shake the guy's hand, and we both would hold one side of the diploma case, while remaining in the handshake for the picture. When my name was called, I walked up to accept my diploma and I got switched around what hand I was supposed to use. I held the diploma with my right hand and awkwardly held the bottom side of this guy's right hand with my left, but at least they pronounced my name right! I sat back down after walking across the stage and I thought about something funny. I was able to graduate even though I did not have the computer class requirements or foreign language requirements I thought I needed, I rolled the dice and won.

Graduation was finally over and it was onto the parking lot to shave my best friend's head clean. After taking pictures with my family, I made my way over to Colby as more people from our group slowly assembled. We decided that all of us would take turns trimming pieces of his hair off. One by one, each of us got the trimmer and tried to trim a strip of hair off. His hair was so thick and long that this electric trimmer would get jammed up and we couldn't go that fast. All of us were laughing hysterically because each pass of the trimmer made Colby look more and more silly. A couple of our friends walked over once they saw what we were doing. It was certainly a show to watch as Mötley Crüe played in the background as we took chunks off of Colby's hair. Finally, the last of the hair was shaved off and Colby looked like a new man. He went from having more hair than a fully grown lion to looking like he enlisted in the military. From there, we headed to Rogers' house to enjoy some post-graduation pizza and get used to Colby's new hair style.

Along with the rainstorm that took out the lights during graduation, we we're supposed to have a graduation party called "Gradfest," where we were allowed to hang out at our school and party all night long with games, food, and a mechanical bull. If you went to Gradfest, you wouldn't have to go to school the next day.

Because it rained so hard during the night of that storm, it flooded my high school and most parts of the city. The river never got that high all year, but it rained so bad that half the city and my high school were almost pool toys. There even was a casino nearby and the water made the first two floors underwater. Our school canceled Gradfest because the water damage was too bad, this made a lot of people upset. I was going to go, but since they had to reschedule it, I wasn't able to because our group had a trip planned on that day. They had drawings to win money during Gradfest and I wasn't sure if I would be able to participate if I didn't go. Coincidentally, I found out that I won 50 bucks and I wasn't even there! I couldn't believe how wild of a week this truly was. The lights went off at my graduation, Gradfest got cancelled because the city's under water, a tornado nearly hit my work, Colby shaved his head, and I won $50. I wish I could say this was made up.

To add to the ongoing chaos, my birthday was two days after we graduated. I would end my last couple of days of high school, being 19 years old. The older I got, I catered to the idea of having fun with my friends from a simple idea. I would much rather go skip rocks on a lake than throw an expensive party. The flooding continued for the next month and water was still up all throughout the city. On the night of my birthday, Colby, Brayden, Jon, Charlie, Zach, Truman, and I all went out on the bridge on the river and watched the flood water flow. This bridge used to be a bridge for cars, but the city turned it into a walking bridge that gave a great view of the river below. We celebrated my birthday as soon as the clock hit midnight while we were on the bridge. A couple of the guys decided to go home soon after, but I still hung out with Truman, Colby, and Zach the rest of the night. We went to go clown around in a town that was on the complete opposite of where we were at. While we were driving around, we saw a flooded soccer field that was near a part of the river. This soccer field was in a low area that allowed water to flow in and remain at waist height. We had the bright idea of wanting to go swim in this water, it was only after the fact that I realized we probably shouldn't have swam in flood water, but it was another in-the-moment decision. We drove up to where it looked like a decent spot to hop in, Zach and I stripped down to our underwear and immediately dove in. Even though it was May, the water was chilly from the past three days of rain. We had our fun laughing and playing in the water for about 20 minutes until we got out. We got dressed, hit the gas station for snacks, and spent the night at Truman's house. My parents later told me I definitely should not have swam in that water and I was not one to argue with them on that. The next day, more of the group met up at Truman's house and we headed to "Pop's," which is a giant soda place along with a restaurant. We had a great time that day by visiting an older motorcycle museum then making our way to Pop's for lunch. This place has every flavor of soda you can think of, even the ones that shouldn't be flavors such as ranch dressing, pickle juice, and barf. The food was absolutely amazing and we loaded up on cases of delicious soda flavors shortly after. We piled back in the car, jamming out to rap and old country songs all the way home. As I mentioned previously, we had already planned a trip on the day that Gradfest was supposed to happen, that was Gridlife. Gridlife is an annual music and drifting festival that's held in certain parts of the country. A couple months prior we had signed up for Gridlife Midwest, hosted at the Gingerman Raceway in South Haven, Michigan. 13 hours and 800 miles away. Haines' sent us videos of how awesome it looked from the previous festivals. Concerts and drifting for three days straight. This was going to be our Senior trip and little did we know it would be the best time of our lives.

15

Gridlife

Five days after my birthday, it was time to venture across the country to the beautiful state of Michigan. A trip that we had been highly anticipating for months was finally here and I was counting down the minutes until we crossed state lines. Eight friends, no parents, 800 miles across the country, this was going to be wild. I got a travel journal for my birthday from my aunt and I figured that was a great opportunity to write down everything that happened during this trip. Most everything in this chapter is pulled from that journal. Some of us spent the night at Truman's the day before we left. I woke up on a chair that morning with Truman nudging me to wake up. I didn't get the best of sleep but eventually as the morning went on I managed to get all my stuff together. Charlie, Colby, Brody, Truman, Matt, Brayden, Haines, and I piled into two cars and were ready for the road. We stopped by QuikTrip one last time before we left town and I was absolutely starving. Everything in there looked delicious to me and I made sure to get a coffee so I wouldn't have a headache on the way to Spencer's house. Our first stop was at Spencer's house in Kansas, there we would hangout for the day and spend the night. As it approached noon, I was in dire need of a Kleenex and I hadn't eaten in hours. When we got Spencer's house, we spent some time driving around the city and even got to drive by Spencer's high school. Since Spencer lived in another state, it was neat to look at the places that were familiar to him. When we returned back to the house, we all gathered in the game room where we took turns playing Forza Motorsport, Rocket League, and Golf. We also got to play with Spencer's dog, Duke, who was elated to see all of us and I couldn't get over how cute he was running around the room. For dinner, Spencer's dad fixed us hamburgers and hot dogs. We sat on the table on the back patio as I had a great dinner with my hamburger, Mountain Dew, and enjoyed the Kansas air. We hadn't seen the sun in about five days and as we sat down to eat at the table, the sun started emerging from the clouds, it was incredible. We wanted to go do something other than stay at the house, we voted to go to a Bass Pro Shops just up the road. I was on the hunt for some clearanced clothes and some of the guys wanted to find straw hats, which is a popular attire for drift events. In Bass Pro, there's this arcade shooting game with mechanical targets when you hit them. We came across this on the second floor and we couldn't help but have a competition on who could score the highest. We all lined up along the benches and took turns one by one trying to hit as many targets within one minute. I did a lot better than I thought, but Matt prevailed victorious after having a near perfect score by the end of his time. On our way out, I noticed a huge rack of clothes on clearance and I picked up an American flag button up shirt. I'd been searching for some classic white guy party apparel and that seemed to fit the criteria. We got back home and resumed playing video games. After four bags of popcorn, I was exhausted by the end of the night and didn't want to face the fact that I'd be waking up in five hours. I crashed on the couch ready to get some sleep, but not before I heard a noise like something was coming up the stairs. Charlie was in the room also and we looked at each other confused. I thought it was the dog but I saw this round shape appear from the depths of the dark staircase. It was Colby and he started to play the song "Un Poco Loco," Charlie and I busted out laughing because that was a funny song amongst our group. After I realized the house wasn't getting burglarized, I was able to fall asleep and look forward to Gridlife the next day!

I woke up bright and early at the sweet time of 6:40 am. I got up fast because I did not want to be the last one packed up. We loaded up the cars and said our last goodbyes to Spencer. We took a polaroid group picture in the driveway and hit the road, 200 miles down with 800 left. My phone was charged, music was going, and all I had to do was mentally prepare myself to go insane for three days straight.

Traffic was fine all the way there until we were on the edge of downtown Chicago. It was bumper to bumper traffic on this eight lane highway in the middle of the day. I've never been in such horrid traffic in my life, moving about 50 yards, every 30 minutes. A few hours went by and we were finally moving faster than a turtle. I blinked my eyes a few times and we had made it to the promised land of South Haven, Michigan. We stopped at a Walmart, where we sorted our tickets out and got some groceries. One of the first things I noticed were all the seagulls in the parking lot. It made sense because the South Beach of Lake Michigan was less than ten minutes away. We slowly made our way to track just before the sun was setting while seeing all these awesome cars go down the street, towards the festival. We drove up to the ticket gate and I was getting a sense of extreme excitement, but it was being held back by the process of signing in, getting our wristbands, and camping stickers. We navigated towards our camp spot while I stuck my head out of the window looking at the cars and listening to the distant rave music, thinking this place looked like a video game. We paid for the better campsite that put us in a great position for all the event activities. The moment when I knew this was going to be a great trip was when our neighbors across the field were playing with a military-grade laser and Jack said to us "I'll see if they can shine it on my nipple." He took off his shirt and we all started yelling, trying to get the attention of the guys with the laser. They snapped the laser in our direction and aimed it perfectly on Jack's nipple, we all were busting a gut as we heard the guys with the laser laughing as well. It took us close to two hours to set up all the tents, tarps, and canopies. By this time, it was fairly late and we decided to call it a night. We got settled in our tents and awaited the next morning that would bring us a full day of drifting, games, and concerts!

I was woken up to the sound of racing engines and pulsing dubstep music early that morning. It was painful getting up, from just how exhausted I was, but I had to remind myself that I just woke up at Gridlife. I got up, got dressed, and made my coffee, before having a small meeting with everyone on what the game plan for the day was. We started off walking around the rows of cars next to our campsite. I've never seen that many Supras, RX-7's, and Skylines all in one place, my camera was about to get a workout. The weather wasn't even close to humid, compared to home, 70 degrees and the sun was shining. We came across a giant beach ball, near one of the clothes stands, that was there for everyone to sign for the concerts later that night. All of us walked over to it and signed the ball with "Tulsa Thot Police." The stands to watch drifting were right next to us, we made our way there and I was able to capture some stunning pictures of the Falken team tearing up the track. We headed back to the campsite later that afternoon to have dinner and relax a bit. We got to talking to our neighbors next to us, one of the guys was named Gabe. Gabe was a super chill guy who befriended Brody and Brayden, then met the rest of us. Gabe and his friends were leaving early that day and he mentioned that there was a cooler full of beer and a handle that he didn't want to haul back home. He and his friends were going somewhere for a bit and he said word-for-word "if that cooler is empty by the time we get back, I won't question what happened." We accepted the offer and subtly thanked him for his generosity. Gabes cooler was now empty and our cooler, which was full of Mountain Dew, had some new friends.

We got word that there was an Xavier Wulf concert later that night, us all being fans of his, were extremely excited. Brayden wasn't too interested in going, hence he opted to stay at the festival. The concert was an hour away in downtown Grand Rapids, but we knew it was worth it. We hopped online and bought tickets right then and there and within minutes, we were unexpectedly going to an Xavier Wulf concert. On the way there we came across an under construction road and were swerving in and out of the cones for about a mile, acting like we were racing at Gridlife. We arrived downtown and I couldn't help but think this place looked similar to downtown Tulsa. We made our way to the venue and I could hear the building rattling from the bass inside. Once inside and past security, I saw a guy with a Lil Peep shirt in the crowd and I knew I was at the right place. I felt the music waving and pulsing through my body, an ecstatic feeling. Concert music makes me feel different than listening to it in a car or on my phone, it's more of a real and vivid experience. It wasn't a big crowd, which I enjoyed because there's a better connection with the artist and the audience. We found a place in the crowd, listened to the openers, and waited for Xavier to come out. Xavier Wulf emerged from backstage and the crowd went crazy, "Idontknowjeffery" also came out alongside him. I couldn't believe that after listening to Xavier's songs during high school, I was able to see him play live, it was surreal. They went through a few songs, getting everyone jumping around and bumping into one another. One of Xavier's more popular songs, "Psycho Pass" came on and Matt and I moved deeper into the crowd. I was going berserk in the mosh pit and then I got slammed into pretty hard, sending me to the ground and hitting my elbow. I knew I had to get up fast, otherwise I'd get trampled by everyone dancing around. I got up, brushed it off, and continued the high energy. At some point, Charlie mentioned he wasn't feeling good and Truman also had a headache, so we stayed for a few more songs, until we eventually departed early. On the way home, I noticed my elbow had swollen up from my fall, but I knew that sometimes mosh pits come with a cost.

On arrival back to the campsite, we noticed that Brayden had taken advantage of our newly acquired drinks from Gabe. Some of the guys were tired from the concert, but Matt, Brody, Jack, Brayden, and I were ready for more concerts. The pulsing EDM music echoed all throughout the festival, getting louder as we got closer. Lasers were shooting everywhere and colorful flashing lights lit up the surroundings. Hundreds of people were gathered by the stage and I was determined to get in the middle of it. I didn't know any of the rave and dubstep artists that were performing, but being there in the environment with tons of other people, conditioned me to enjoy it as much as a die-hard fan. I made it a goal to go to the concerts every night we were there so I could experience all I could. I tried to put myself in a state of complete happiness by not focusing on anything else but the feeling of the music. I thought the songs were great and it wasn't hard to dance along with everyone in the strobing lights. After an hour or two, we went back to the campsite where we all met up and wanted to play the game "Paranoia." It's where we all sit in a circle and a person whispers a question to someone next to them such as "who would be most likely to get a felony?" The person who got asked, says the name out loud, then a coin is flipped. If it's tails, the person who said the name, has to say what the question was, if it's heads, the question is not to be revealed, making everyone paranoid. The game was even more entertaining because half the group was making a dent on the cooler, this caused the questions to be more ridiculous and more feelings got hurt. After some of the guys went to bed, I still had some energy in me to go back out to the festival. Brody, Matt, and I headed back out just as it was close to 1 am. There was a silent disco party going on near the main stage, where everyone had headphones dancing along with no outside music and a DJ on top of a bus. We grabbed pairs of headphones and joined in on the party. Silent discos are one of the most unique ways to enjoy music. When the headphones are on, it sounds like you're at a loud concert and the person next to you is hearing the same music, but if you take the headphones off, it's complete silence. Next to the silent disco area was a tent full of drifting simulator video games, with steering wheels and racing chairs. Brody and I walked over there and played around on the video games for a while, still wearing the silent disco headphones. It was now close to 3 am. Fatigue started to set in and my body was telling me it was time to get some sleep, even if I may not have wanted to. We slowly made our way back to the tent for the final time that night. I got cozy in my sleeping bag and I could tell I was going to sleep well that night.

The next morning almost repeated itself, as far as the engine noises and rave music, but I woke up to a soaking wet sleeping bag because I left the tent screen unzipped and it had rained that night. I wasn't too upset because there was nothing I could change besides hoping it would dry out by the time I went to bed. Unfortunately, it would be raining the rest of that day, but nonetheless the drifting continued. It didn't affect the track that much and the drivers were skilled enough to where they could adapt to track conditions. A couple of the guys were able to do a ride-along, where they paid to secure a spot with one of the drivers for a run on the track. Brody got to ride in a 2JZ motor swapped Subaru WRX Impreza that did a 360 degree drift on the rainy track.

I was in the stands taking pictures and I saw Brody's car come around the corner, then suddenly the driver threw the steering wheel and the car did a perfect 360, while still continuing the drift, I was beyond impressed. Food trucks, buying clothes, and walking around is what the middle of the day entailed. The rain had mostly cleared up and we thought that was the end of it, until later that evening when it started to look a little spooky outside. The clouds were getting darker and the wind was picking up. There was a dense storm cloud above the festival, with a ring of light and white clouds just above the horizon. The winds intensified even more and people began to shift their focus from the festival to getting back to their campsite. We began making our way back to the tents to make sure nothing would blow away, as we saw others running as well. On our way back, we saw multiple tents and canopies being lifted up and tossed across the sky like they were tissues being blown around. It was quite scary thinking there could easily be a tornado forming right in front of us, but it was equally thrilling. We made it back to the tents and luckily they were still adhered to the ground, but not for long. We all grab hold of our tents, canopy, and anything that could blow away. I saw the clouds rapidly moving in the sky and the darkness fading along with it. About 20 minutes later, the wind was dying down and the sky looked less intimidating. Once we knew that the car wouldn't become a frisbee, we were able to continue on with the festival.

Later that night, we returned to the main stage. There were more well-known artists on this third night, one of them was Oliver Tree. Some of the guys were familiar with him, but I had no idea who he was. His music has the style of punk rock, with rap and pop mixed in it. At first I didn't like it, but after a few songs, I warmed up to his music. There was one song where he got everyone hyped up and made a mosh pit. Usually I would hop in, but this one looked brutal. Huge guys were pushing each other, punching, Matt and I even saw a guy get body-slammed into the mud. I felt like I was watching a football scrimmage as this guy's glowstick flew off when he hit the ground. The dubstep songs seemed better than they were the previous night as they played many of my favorite mixes. As I'm dancing along, I look up and see that there's a group of guys carrying a cardboard car, made out of beer cases and duck tape, through the middle of the crowd. It had wheels, doors, and a steering wheel, it was one of the best things I'd seen all trip. We also saw the giant beach ball with everyone's signature being thrown all in the crowd. It eventually made its way over to us, where I saw where we had signed it earlier that day. It was around midnight when we left the concert and headed back to the tents. It was the last night of the trip and we wanted to make sure we made use of all our food and drinks. One of the guys had a decent amount to drink from the handle and decided it was time to make sandwiches for everyone, though I wasn't complaining because I was starving after all that dancing. He struggled to situate the buns on the plates and keep the pan from falling over on the small propane stove. At one point, he hit the stove and the bacon flew all over the table and onto the ground. I was laughing extremely hard. A friendly family came over to us and asked what we were doing and we explained that our friend was making sandwiches, then our friend offered to make the family one, keep in mind that it's 1 in the morning. They said yes and our friend started to make the sandwich. Jack and I were standing by as we saw him barely put the bacon on the pan. While we were talking to this family, they explained to us that this was their second year coming and they planned on going the next as well. Our friend was able to put the sandwich together and gave it to the family. The mom handed it to their young daughter and said "can you say thank you to the man for making you a sandwich?" In her little kid voice, she thanked our friend and the family headed off. I've always wondered if that family knew if our friend was sober or not, because that was no doubt one of the funniest parts of the trip. We even had a falling asleep contest between Charlie and Brayden on who could fall asleep first. We sounded off a countdown and on "Go!" We see Brayden run, slip, and dive into his tent. My stomach was aching from laughing so hard from everything that night.

The next morning was our last day at Gridlife and it was surely the best weather of the trip so far, it was clear skies, sunny and 60 degrees. We watched the last couple of the drift events that were going on and we got to meet a bunch of famous drifters like Adam

LZ, Vaughn Gittin Jr., Ryan Turek, Chelsea Denofa, and many others. Later on that afternoon, we were taking down the campsite and we were all exhausted. All of us had barely any sleep that entire trip and we were running off of girl scout cookies, mountain dew, homemade sandwiches, and Gabe's drinks. We sprawled out on the air mattresses to deflate them and I remember laying there with a Mountain Dew in one hand and Tagalongs in the other thinking, man I really don't want to leave. We packed everything up and headed out of the festival as we kissed Gridlife goodbye. On our way out of Michigan, we made sure to stop by South Beach. I could see why it's called one of the Great Lakes, because Lake Michigan looked exactly like an ocean, never seeming to end in every direction. People were playing in the water, seagulls were everywhere, and I even saw someone parasailing with a wakeboard. We then made the long journey back home. It was much longer of a trip heading back than it was going there. We made our way to the wonderful city of St. Louis to spend the night. As we were pulling up, I thought it looked like New York City with all the lights and many unique buildings. I've never been to NYC, but this is what I imagined it looks like. We also passed the capitol building that was on the way to our hotel. Once we got inside and got settled, I felt my sunburn start to take its toll. I had such a bad sunburn that day, I went out in the hallway with Truman, standing underneath the air conditioning, letting the cool air run across my back. Nothing felt better than that sense of pain paired with a soothing cool breeze. That was the first time I was nauseated from a sunburn and it was difficult to fall asleep that night.

I had the best sleep of the entire trip in that hotel and my sunburn seemed to no longer affect me when I woke up. The Gateway Arch was right outside our window, thus we planned to go visit it after we checked out that morning. We went to the Gateway Arch Museum and read about the history that led up to the construction of it. We were going to take the tour up to the top, but it was at 12:30 and we had to be out of there by at most 11:30. The Arch was still very fascinating, being able to walk up to the base and gaze up at its colossal size. Back to the car we went, as we waved The Gateway Arch goodbye and set the route back to the house.

The everlasting feeling of coasting on the highway carried me all the way home. It was cloudy the entire way there, almost like the weather knew I was bummed about heading back home. The car tire's rolled into Truman's driveway as we made it back to the homeland in one piece. It was a wild journey and I enjoyed every second of it. I saw so many things, did so many things, and the music was phenomenal. Deep down I knew that the party wouldn't last forever and I'd have to go back to school and work, but there is no doubt that I tried my hardest to get the most out of that trip and I believed I succeeded. Yes I destroyed my elbow, yes my sleeping bag was soaking wet that morning, and yes I had a bone-numbing sunburn, but that just added to the experience of this trip and that's all I could've asked for. While dancing by the stage, feeling the music and engine noises radiating through my body, I closed my eyes and thought that no one else is experiencing my type of exhilaration and a heightened sense of euphoria than I was in that moment I was there...that was empowering.

I thought about a lot of things on the way home. School had ended, college was starting, and many of my friends who I saw everyday, I may never see again. Some were going into the military, film school, and Nascar school, yes, you read that right. But one thing I'll always remember is how I spent my time during high school. I wasn't a championship football player or the star baseball pitcher that got all the girls, but I could look at myself in the mirror and know I wasn't lying to myself about who I was or what I wanted in life. I not only had some self-fulfilling adventures, but I was able to share it with others for the same reason.

I am thankful to be a part of a group of buds I can call my second family. Those four years of high school were the best years of school I'd ever had. Backing into my parking spot every morning, lined up next to my friends all in the back of the parking lot. Spontaneous trips to downtown and other states, the adventures never ended. We have all truly lived life to the fullest as a group and I couldn't be happier any other way. As Andy Bernard from *The Office* once said "I wish there was a way to know you're in the good old days before you've actually left them." It's a time to have great memories and bond with people who you might not expect to bond with. It's the middle ground of being a kid and adult, these experiences from these years will help shape the person you become. Don't think not being in sports or having a large circle of friends will doom you to a life of boredom, you have to take control and make those wanted experiences happen. That reminds me how later that concept led me to quit my job, cut my hair, and buy a travel van; or the time where our group had strippers show up to our Halloween party, and even when I ran in a 15k race with the flu…but…I'll leave that for another story.

Acknowledgments

It's crazy to think that each person I've come across in my life has led me to where I am today. The people I met in elementary school led me to meet new people in middle school and thus led me to those I met in high school. It was a web of infinite directions I could've gone down but it shaped into what this book has become. I am thankful for God for getting me through the hardest times with battling anxiety to get this book written. I wrote this book in secret with none of my friends or family knowing. I know they will be excited and proud that I've accomplished this, knowing that brings me complete happiness.

I can't emphasize enough that if my senior year English teacher Mr. Acebo, never assigned that end of the year assignment, this book probably wouldn't have been written. I want to personally thank all the members of my friend group for being there all those years and taking part in some of the craziest memories from high school. Thank you, Jon, Jackson, Truman, Brody, Brayden, Colby, Zach, Rogers, Jack H., Jack M., Charlie, Matt, Spencer, viva la TTP. There are many other people that came and went throughout the years and they're certainly not forgotten. I also want to thank Vivien Reis for helping me with the cover design and her efforts in perfecting this book with me.

About the Author

Nick Umbarger is a college student from Tulsa, Oklahoma. An aspiring entrepreneur with thundering ambitions in the automotive and business world. Nick is also a skateboarder, photographer, fishermen, traveler, mechanic, and professional fun-haver. When he's not doing schoolwork or spending time with his family, you can find him swinging in a hammock by a waterfall or finding the best new music for his ever-evolving playlists. Visit him on Instagram @nickumbarger_

CPSIA information can be obtained
at www.ICGtesting.com
Printed in the USA
LVHW092248140821
695340LV00007B/258/J